D0000858

FAMILY CAMPING
COOKBOOK

FAMILY CAMPING COOKBOOK

Tiff & Jim Easton

DUNCAN BAIRD PUBLISHERS

LONDON

FAMILY CAMPING COOKBOOK
Tiff & Jim Easton

Distributed in the USA and Canada by
Sterling Publishing Co., Inc.
387 Park Avenue South
New York, NY 10016-8810

This edition published in USA in 2013 by
Duncan Baird Publishers, an imprint of
Watkins Publishing Limited
75 Wells Street
London W1T 3QH

A member of Osprey Group

Copyright © Watkins Publishing Limited 2012,
2013
Text copyright © Tiff and Jim Easton 2012,
2013
For copyright of photographs see page 176
which is to be regarded as an extension
of this copyright.

The right of Tiff and Jim Easton to be
identified as the Authors of this text has been
asserted in accordance with the Copyright,
Designs and Patents Act of 1988.

All rights reserved. No part of this book
may be reproduced in any form or by any
electronic or mechanical means, including
information storage and retrieval systems,
without permission in writing from the
publisher, except by a reviewer who may
quote brief passages in a review.

Managing Editor: Grace Cheetham
Editors: Krissy Mallett and Joanna Smith
Managing Designer: Luana Gobbo
Production: Uzma Taj
Commissioned photography: Ed Easton

ISBN: 978-1-84899-089-0

10 9 8 7 6 5 4 3 2 1

Typeset in Claredon and Meta
Color reproduction by Colourscan
Printed in China

To Joanie, Beck and Remy

Publisher's note: While every care has
been taken in compiling the recipes for this
book, Watkins Publishing Limited, or any
other persons who have been involved in
working on this publication, cannot accept
responsibility for any errors or omissions,
inadvertent or not, that may be found in the
recipes or text, nor for any problems that may
arise as a result of preparing one of these
recipes. If you are pregnant or breastfeeding
or have any special dietary requirements or
medical conditions, it is advisable to consult
a medical professional before following any
of the recipes contained in this book. Some
foraged ingredients such as wild mushrooms
can be fatally poisonous, however you cook
them. Neither the publisher nor the authors
can take any responsibility for any illness or
other unintended consequences resulting from
following any of the advice or suggestions in
this book.

Unless otherwise stated:
• Use extra large eggs
• Use medium fruit and vegetables
• Use fresh ingredients, including herbs and
  chilies
• Use fish and shellfish caught via sustainable
  farming methods
• 1 tsp. = 5ml   1 tbsp. = 15ml   1 cup = 240ml

Acknowledgments: Thank you to Ed for the
fantastic photographs, to Maddy, Lucas and
Ruben for all their help, enthusiasm and
patience, to our parents for their inspiration,
and to our family and friends who have all
helped us along the way. Thank you also to
Camping Les Clots in the Tarn Valley, and
the exceedingly family-friendly campground,
Mathevies, in the Dordogne, and Gags in
our beloved West Wittering, for the fantastic
locations for many of our photos. And
lastly, thank you also to Grace Cheetham for
commissioning the book, Luana Gobbo for
making the book look so lovely, Krissy Mallett
for being so thorough and so patient with us
at the final stages of editing, and of course
to Clare Hulton who got the ball rolling in the
first place.

Contents

Introduction

Cooking in the outdoors is one of life's great pleasures, a chance to release your inner caveman, but with better ingredients. And of course, it is an indisputable fact that food tastes great eaten outside. So, while canned beans and barbecued sausages have their place, a collection of simple, inspiring and delicious recipes can transform the culinary camping experience.

To be clear, we are not talking about freeze-dried cheese on the north face of the Eiger, biltong in the Kalahari, collapsible forks or titanium cooking vessels. If you are anything like us, it is more likely to be a farm campground with children and a few pots and pans from home. You may have to compromise on sleeping comfort, and you may have to take cold showers, but if you can eat decent meals, cooked by your own hand, all will be well.

We spend a large part of our family camping trips thinking of good things to eat, and devising new ways of preparing and cooking them. Camping is about simplicity, being outdoors and making a virtue of everyday activities. Away from the hectic logistics of cooking for a family at home, outdoor cooking becomes an unfettered, everyday adventure in which the whole family can participate. Kids love to get involved and will probably become more adventurous in their eating habits than at home.

This book is drawn from our own camping experiences and from our circle of fellow camping friends and family. The premise is simple: you have a car, a cooler with some ice, a portable barbecue or metal grill rack for using over an open fire, a single-burner camping stove and the items listed in the Equipment section (pages 16–17). You also bring a small selection of ingredients to expand your camping culinary repertoire. We have also set out the Camping Storecupboard (pages 12–13) and devised 12 meal plans for camping trips, to make it easy for you to organize your trip.

ABOUT THIS BOOK

The main rule when cooking outdoors is that there are not too many rules. It is not about precision or perfection, but having fun while cooking good, simple food. Every recipe in this book works for all types of cooking equipment—whether it's a portable barbecue, camping stove or a metal grill rack over an open fire—and the recipes accommodate the different cooking times. All the recipes have been tried and tested in the outdoors by us, our family and many of our friends.

We've divided the book into four chapters. "Quick Escapes" is for when you make a sudden decision to go camping for a weekend and don't have much time to gather together a long list of ingredients. "By the Beach" has recipes that radiate sunshine, using lots of fresh, summer produce and delicious seafood. "In the Country" has heartier recipes featuring meat, cheese and eggs, and all the good things you can get from the fresh vegetable and fruit stand or from the farmers' market. The final chapter, "Festivals & Parties," has recipes for camping with a large, hungry group. For each chapter, we have included a list of key ingredients. So if you are going off for a week by the beach, for example, you should take what you can from the list in that chapter along with you. Each chapter also has some tips to help you along the way and three different meal plans. The first is geared toward young kids, the second toward older kids and the third toward vegetarians.

Although we have given precise quantities for every recipe, they are not the sort of recipes that require absolute precision. We've tried to make sure that you can measure nearly everything with a handful, a cup, a teaspoon or a tablespoon, and that more complicated measurements can be worked out roughly from the packaging your food is bought in. We have also tried to make the recipes versatile so that most of the ingredients can be substituted for something similar, depending on what you have available.

Food and Ingredients

A little bit of planning goes a long way on a family camping trip, especially where food is concerned. The trick is to take enough ingredients with you to give you flexibility with cooking and eating options, but not so much that you need to buy a bigger car to get it there!

Thinking about what you want to cook and eat when you get there is also a good idea. At the beginning of each chapter we have included three meal plans, complete with shopping lists. These have been designed to minimize the number of ingredients you need to pack. They are weekend plans so that you can take and keep all the ingredients listed for the two days with a cooler and a modicum of preparation. If you're going for a week or longer, you can start with a weekend plan and then you can simply combine meal plans and add whichever recipes you'd like.

Good ingredients can make all the difference, particularly when you are keeping things simple. Canned tomatoes are a cheap ingredient, so it's worth buying the best you can get—the difference in taste and texture is huge! Similarly with meat, it's worth paying a bit over the odds for better quality, particularly if you are barbecuing. Useful ingredients are those that keep well in packs, like halloumi cheese (which is fantastic grilled), and it's also worth remembering to use fresh ingredients that don't require a lot of cleaning, like bananas and avocados.

BUYING BEFORE YOU LEAVE VS BUYING LOCALLY

What you take with you from home and what you buy locally will be determined by how long you are going for, what you can get when you get there and how much of a rush you leave in. We find it best to take the core ingredients with us, but still have the flexibility to buy a leg of lamb from a farmers' market, or some fresh line-caught fish from a shack on the beach. Certainly for the first day or two, it's easier to have some certainty and take food with you.

FORAGING

Like camping itself, gathering wild ingredients helps you to connect with nature. What you can forage for depends enormously on where you are, but with a little effort and local knowledge it is immensely satisfying and great fun!

At the beach, look out for wild arugula, which tends to grow in dry borders. This lovely peppery leaf is delicious in salads or sandwiches like Lomo a la Plancha, which are crispy pork ciabattas (page 35). Samphire, commonly found in salt-marshes and mangroves, tastes magical with fish. Try it steamed with some asparagus alongside the Grilled Fish & Smoky Eggplant Salad (page 84). If you feel confident, you can also forage for mussels and clams along the beach and even go shrimping. Even a small haul can go a long way and will make for a superior Seafood Linguine (page 83).

If you are in woodland you can often find wild garlic (ramps). The leaves have a similar taste to chives and are perfect for adding to omelets or rice dishes—try it in Risotto Primavera (page 126). You might find some wild sorrel, which has a distinctive lemony flavor and can make the most mouthwatering sauces to liven up fish or chicken dishes. Wild fennel, which you'll find beside trails and roadsides in California, is also lovely added to pork and is a good substitute for fennel seeds if you don't have any. Wild mint (field mint) and parsley can also commonly be found, as can rosemary, oregano and thyme.

There is also plenty of fruit to be foraged—apples, plums, blackberries, figs, all of which would make a brilliant Foil Fruit Cobbler (page 57). And then, of course, there are mushrooms, but we only advise foraging for these if you have some expertise in identifying the edible varieties. If you have the know-how, the Herby Wild Mushrooms (page 109) recipe is a must!

However, it's not a free-for-all, and there are some basic principles to remember. Make sure you are allowed to collect or pick from your surroundings before heading off into the wilderness and never pick more than you need. It's always extremely important to have some way of correctly identifying what you pick as some very edible plants and mushrooms have some poisonous lookalikes. A detailed guide book with pictures is vital.

The Camping Storecupboard

You can (and should) take more ingredients, sauces and spices than you might initially think you'll need. They are probably sitting in your cupboard and mostly come in small jars, bottles or cans. A small box of carefully selected ingredients will expand your cooking repertoire enormously, and you should be able to smuggle them into the car somewhere.

It's easy to be dismissive of canned foods. Like all things, some canned foods are not good, while others are more convenient and no less tasty than their fresh equivalents. Canned legumes are great, and much more practical than dried legumes, as the water and heat required to soak and cook dried ones does not lend itself well to camping. However, although canned legumes are good, canned vegetables are generally not, except perhaps for tomatoes, which are often great if you are making a sauce. Many "canned" tomatoes now come in cartons if you need to keep weight to a minimum.

Throughout this book, we have tried to use short lists of key ingredients that can be used for a wide range of recipes. You may be able to buy food locally, but you really want to avoid spending the first day of your camping trip in a supermarket. We recommend taking the following items and buying the rest of your ingredients locally.

MUST-HAVES

- bouillon cubes
- chili sauce or dried chili flakes
- garam masala
- garlic
- ginger root
- lemons
- Marinade Base (page 21)
- olive oil
- salt and pepper
- soy sauce
- sugar and/or honey
- Vinaigrette (page 21)

GOOD TO HAVE

- allspice, ground
- cinnamon
- cumin, ground
- limes
- oregano, dried
- smoked paprika

IN THE COOLER

- butter
- herbs, fresh (such as cilantro leaves, mint leaves and parsley leaves)
- milk
- your first meal (page 19)

USEFUL CANS & JARS

- canned chickpeas and other legumes such as lentils, cannellini beans or kidney beans
- canned diced tomatoes
- canned tuna
- harissa paste
- olives
- relishes and condiments, such a eggplant relish, ketchup, mango chutney and mustard
- strawberry or apricot jam

USEFUL DRY INGREDIENTS

- basmati rice
- chocolate
- couscous
- dried fruit
- marshmallows
- noodles
- pasta
- soft flour tortillas
- unsalted nuts

Cooking in the Outdoors

There are a few principles to bear in mind when cooking in the outdoors. First is to always use your heat wisely. Save boiled water to do your dish-washing, and always make the most of the heat on a portable barbecue or campfire. We often cook some meat for our next day's lunch on the grill the night before, and have even used pasta cooking water to fill our hot water bottles!

Second is to make sure you take the right pans to cook in. Many of the recipes in this book can be cooked in one pan and never need more than two. Whether you are cooking on a camping stove, portable barbecue or on an open fire, if your pans are large enough and have a heavy bottom, you'll find they will work whether you are boiling, frying or grilling your food.

It's good to remember that whatever your cooking source, it is less controllable than your stove at home and probably not as hot. So boiling large quantities of water for long periods should be avoided. For best results when pan-frying, work in small batches because overcrowding the skillet will cool it down. A pan lid is indispensable as it speeds up cooking times. It's also worth remembering that the weather can affect cooking times. In cooler, gustier weather, the flames are not as hot or intense as on still, warm days.

CAMPING STOVES

Most of the time you will probably be cooking on a camping stove. There are many different varieties, from single-burner versions in their own carrying case to multi-burner stoves. A single-burner stove is good to take to the beach, but if you are camping and cooking regularly then a double-burner version is better. Some have a burner and a grill, with the grill next to the burner, and with a lid that doubles as a wind-shield—important because even a light breeze can slow down cooking times noticeably. If you don't have this feature, cook behind (but not too close to) some kind of makeshift windbreak. You can normally choose between butane, propane and Coleman fuel (also known as white gas or Naptha). If you're only taking a stove, make sure you take a grill pan with you so you can grill over the flame.

PORTABLE BARBECUES

Portable barbecues are an essential part of the camping experience. Although open fires aren't always allowed in campgrounds, barbecues normally are. If your campground allows, you can build your own barbecue with bricks or stones and a simple metal grill rack. Otherwise a simple, low portable barbecue should do the trick—there is a huge choice out there, including folding ones. Most pots and pans can be used on a barbecue as long as you don't mind them blackening on the outside. Cast-iron pots are probably best, but there are many other lighter varieties available. The good thing about a portable barbecue—especially if you have the bucket type—is that once you have finished cooking, you can turn it into a campfire simply by adding some wood. Disposable barbecue grills are no substitute for the real thing—they generally don't get as hot and burn out too quickly.

OPEN FIRES

We always try to seek out campgrounds that allow open fires. Cooking on open fires offers endless possibilities: you can fry, boil, grill, roast and even bake on them, but it does require a bit of practice and the right equipment. A good big metal grill rack, ideally with feet to stand over the embers, is essential, and pots, pans and tea kettles with handles that don't melt are also a good idea. If you are cooking meat, fish or vegetables directly over the fire, as you do on a barbecue, you should wait until the flames have died down and you have glowing embers to cook on. If you are cooking in a saucepan or boiling a tea kettle, you can cook over the flames, but they will tarnish the outside of the pots so don't take your best set. A selection of good-sized stones are useful for supporting the pots and pans in the fire. And for fire safety reasons it goes without saying that you should always have a bucket of water to hand when cooking over an open fire or a portable barbecue. For tips on how to build and light an open fire, see page 99.

Equipment

You don't need to buy lots of specialist camping equipment as most of the things you need will already be in your kitchen. More important is to take the right things, and not too many of them. We have included a checklist below of the critical items—and with these you can prepare and cook everything in this book. Unless you're solely using a grill pan for cooking, most of the desserts in the meal plans are prepared using different cooking equipment from the main course in order to avoid dish-washing midway through a meal.

THE COOLER

This is a must-have. A good, sealable cooler is as important as a means to store food away from roaming animals as it is a place to keep food cold. We always leave ours outside the tent with some frozen food in it to keep other food cold while it slowly defrosts. And if you don't have any frozen food, it's worth knowing that most campgrounds have ice vending machines. Good cooler management can keep food and drinks cold for days. Don't forget to keep your cooler and its contents clean and cool at all times.

THE CUTTING BOARD

This is an excellent work surface, so bring as big a board as possible. Use one side for meat and the other for fruit and vegetables.

POTS AND PANS

We've tried in these recipes to ensure the minimum use of pans, and if you are planning a whole meal, make sure that you don't need the same skillet for your dessert as you used for your sausages.

FOOD BAGS

Plastic food or freezer bags are an absolute must-have for marinating meat, mixing and crushing. Don't forget them. It saves space and is incredibly effective; you can really rub the marinade in once the bag is sealed. It also involves no dish-washing, which is definitely a good thing when you're camping!

EQUIPMENT CHECKLIST

- bottle opener
- bowls
- campfire grill rack
- camping stove and fuel
- can opener
- cheese grater
- cooler
- cutlery
- cutting board (large)
- dishpan and dish-washing liquid, sponge scrubber and dish cloth
- dish towels
- firestarters and matches
- grill pan—if you don't plan to barbecue or cook over an open fire
- grill tongs
- knife, very sharp
- lanterns or candles
- lid to fit both your skillet and saucepan (multi-size)
- measuring cup
- mugs
- paper towels
- pastry brush
- pitcher (large)
- plastic freezer bags or zip-lock bags (large)
- plastic mixing bowl or Tupperware container with a lid (large)
- plates
- portable grill and fuel
- potato peeler
- saucepan (large)
- scrub brush—for cleaning vegetables
- skillet (large)
- spatula
- tinfoil (lots)
- trash bags
- water carrier
- wooden skewers (lots)
- wooden spoons (2)

The First Night

The first day of a family camping trip is usually the most intense: you arrive with limited daylight hours in a race to put up your tent, get water and generally get organized while placating tired, hungry or overexcited children. Then you have to think about dinner. From bitter experience it is best to do this the other way around, so a bit of preparation pays off enormously.

There are various levels of preparation: you can bring a fully prepared meal, ready to go as soon as you are, or at the other extreme a set of ingredients to prepare and assemble once you have set up camp.

For us the hybrid model works best. Have a barbecue on the first night and you will know you are truly camping (a good way of banishing the post-journey and set-up stresses), but also prepare a hearty cold side dish the night before you leave and take it with you in the cooler. Potato salads are excellent because they seem to improve overnight in the fridge and are very quick and easy to make.

Couscous and rice also don't take long to prepare, so if you have time to bring the meat for recipes such as the Lebanese Kebabs (page 41) or the Sticky Ribs (page 159) in the cooler already in their marinades, they make great first-nighters too. If there's any part of the meal that you could prepare in advance to ease the first-night madness, like the Cucumber Raita for the Chicken Tikka (page 160), don't hesitate. It will be more than worth it!

If you can't barbecue or don't feel like it, all the recipes will be just as rewarding cooked on a grill pan on a camping stove. Other particularly quick and easy meals to prepare on a portable stove include the Tomatoes & Chickpeas with Couscous (page 50) and the Cashew Stir-Fry (page 51).

Our favorite first-night meal is Grilled Pork Chops with German Potato Salad (page 81). We light the portable barbecue near the end of setting up, or about 35 to 45 minutes before we want to eat. On go the chops once the coals are ready, out comes the salad from the cooler and the camping trip has begun!

Prepare Ahead

It's not only helpful to prepare ahead for the first night, it's also worth making up some marinades and dressings and even some dry mixtures before you leave. Not only will you be prepared for each meal, but it will also save you packing large quantities of ingredients like flours and spices that you might not need.

For that reason we have used the Prepare Ahead symbol, to indicate how you might be able to get organized in advance. The symbol below will appear on the recipe pages to give you hints and tips on what and how to prepare ahead. It will also appear next to the recipe titles on the meal plans to let you know when an element of the recipe can be prepared ahead of time. For example, when you see the Prepare Ahead symbol next to the Blueberry Pancakes with Maple Syrup recipe on the first 'By the Beach' meal plan (page 63), you'll know to take a look at the recipe to see what you can do to prepare at home. In this case, it's as simple as measuring up and combining dry ingredients, but you can often make up marinades or even whole salads in advance.

There are two extremely important and useful recipes that we definitely think you should make up at home. The first is a delicious balsamic Vinaigrette, which works well with nearly all of our salad dishes. The recipe for this appears on the page opposite and makes enough to fill a generous 2 cups plastic bottle. Don't worry if you don't use it all as it lasts for up to one month and can be finished off at home. The second is a simple Marinade Base, made with lemon juice and garlic. Having a small plastic bottle of this handy will also prove invaluable, particularly as it's quite fiddly to have to squeeze lemons and crush garlic on site. This marinade is also the base for nearly all our marinades, and the variations are listed opposite.

 Prepare ahead: You'll find this symbol on the recipe pages and meal plans whenever you can make part of your meal at home before you leave.

Basic Recipes

Vinaigrette

PREPARATION TIME: 5 MINUTES

generous 1⅓ cups olive oil scant ¾ cup balsamic 1 teaspoon Dijon mustard
vinegar salt and pepper

1 Put the oil and balsamic vinegar in a container with a lid. Add the mustard, then secure with a lid and shake vigorously until well combined. Season with salt and pepper to taste.

Marinade Base

This recipe makes enough for one week's camping as long as you store it in the cooler. It can be used to make a range of different marinades, but if you decide to make the Indian, Thai or Chinese variations below, it's best to use limes instead of lemons.

PREPARATION TIME: 10 MINUTES

juice of 5 lemons
5 garlic cloves, crushed

1 Put the lemon juice, garlic and any variation ingredients, if using, in a jam jar. Secure with a lid and shake vigorously until well combined.

VARIATIONS
Per 1 tablespoon of marinade base:
Spanish: add a pinch of smoked paprika
Moroccan: add a pinch of ground cumin
Lebanese: add a pinch each of ground allspice and cinnamon
Indian: add a pinch of garam masala, 1 tablespoon yogurt and 1 handful of chopped cilantro leaves
Thai: add a splash of Thai fish sauce, 1 tablespoon grated ginger root and 1 handful of chopped cilantro leaves
Chinese: add a splash of soy sauce and 1 tablespoon grated ginger root

QUICK
ESCAPES

Quick Escapes

This chapter is all about being spontaneous and seizing the moment. The sun is shining and you make a last-minute decision to head off with your tent. The recipes here capture this spirit of adventure. With planning time at a minimum, simplicity is key, so most of the recipes have a short list of ingredients which you may already have at home, or which are easy to find in a local store.

If you only have half an hour, take as much as you can from the list below and you will have all the basic storecupboard ingredients you'll need. If you have a little longer, have a quick look at the meal plans and make the most of the ready-to-use shopping lists.

Many of the recipes are also very quick to prepare, making them ideal for a late arrival on site. Some of the meals, like our delicious Tomatoes & Chickpeas with Couscous (page 50), can be rustled up in minutes. This chapter also celebrates the discerning shortcut. Chicken Satay Skewers & Asian Salad (page 47) is a family favorite and demonstrates the magic that can be worked from a humble jar of peanut butter and a few other ingredients.

Even on an impromptu weekend camping trip without much preparation or equipment, there is lots here for children to get involved in and enjoy. Our kids love making up tinfoil packages, preparing skewers or stuffing bananas with chocolate and marshmallows, and the Toffee Apple Crepes (page 54) are always a hit!

KEY INGREDIENTS

- allspice, ground
- bouillon cubes
- chili sauce
- ginger root
- herbs, fresh (bay leaves, mint leaves, parsley leaves and thyme sprigs)
- olive oil and/or sunflower oil
- salt and pepper
- soy sauce
- sugar and/or honey
- Vinaigrette (page 21)

TIPS

Get the kids involved

As we all know from bitter experience, there's nothing worse than spending hours cooking up something delicious and presenting it to your children, only for them to reject it without even trying it. Camping provides the ideal opportunity to have your kids help with the cooking, and once they're involved, you'll be amazed at how adventurous they'll become. Get them to put the meat, fish, halloumi or fruit onto skewers for barbecuing and all of a sudden it becomes something interesting and enticing to eat. You can have them make their own tinfoil packages of food to roast on the fire: chicken, vegetables, fish and even fruit—it all works a treat. There's also a lot of enjoyment to be had molding burgers, rolling up Gorp Balls and choosing fillings for crepes and quesadilla calzones. Cooking together and having fun with food is also the perfect way to encourage their eating habits—and if this is something you struggle with at home, you may find it much easier in the relaxed environment of the campsite.

The cooler

Refrigeration is always tricky when camping, but if you're careful you'll manage fine with a large cooler, certainly for a weekend. Here are a few tips to managing your cooler and keeping it cool:

1 Take as much as you can frozen from home. We even freeze our milk and juices beforehand, and they work as fantastic ice blocks.
2 Pack as much ice as you can into your cooler and ensure everything in the cooler is well-wrapped and waterproofed in case the ice melts. Many campgrounds have ice vending machines, too.
3 Cold air sinks, so it's best to put frozen ingredients at the top of the cooler. Just make sure that the ingredients you put at the top won't leak as they defrost.
4 If you want to keep large quantities of drinks very cold for at least one night, then a bag of ice and a bucket is the way to go.

🍴 Meal Plan for Young Kids

FRIDAY DINNER	• Lebanese Kebabs with Chickpea Salad (page 41) 🏠 • Banana, Chocolate & Marshmallow Boats (page 56)
SATURDAY BREAKFAST	• Oatmeal with Bananas & Honey (page 30)
SATURDAY LUNCH	• Spanish Tortilla (page 39)
SATURDAY DINNER	• Chicken, Tomato & Rosemary Packages (page 45) • Foil Fruit Cobbler (page 57)
SUNDAY BREAKFAST	• Grandpa's Eggs (page 33)
SUNDAY LUNCH	• Sardine Pâté (page 38)

SHOPPING LIST

Spices & Flavorings
allspice, ground (½ tsp.)
honey (1 jar)
olive oil (1 bottle)
salt & pepper
sugar, brown (½ cup)

Cans & Jars
chickpeas (14½ oz.)
sardines (1 tin)

Dry Foods
bread, crusty (½ loaf)
marshmallows (1 bag)
milk chocolate (3½ oz.)
pita breads (8)
rolled oats (3¼ cups)

Meat
chicken breast filets (4)
lamb leg (1 lb. 5 oz.)

Chilled Foods
butter (2¼ sticks)
cream cheese (8 oz.)
eggs, extra large (8)
milk (1 pint)
yogurt, thick plain (1 cup)

Fruit & Vegetables
apples (3)
bananas (8)
carrots (2)
cucumbers (1½)
garlic cloves (4)
lemons (4)
new potatoes (3 lb.)
onions (2)
parsley leaves (2 handfuls)
rosemary sprigs, small (4)
tomatoes (6)

🍴 Meal Plan for Older Kids

FRIDAY DINNER	• Chicken Satay Skewers & Asian Salad (page 47) • Barbecued Pineapple Wedges (page 53)
SATURDAY BREAKFAST	• Eggy Bread with Bacon & Tomatoes (page 32)
SATURDAY LUNCH	• Lomo a la Plancha (page 35)
SATURDAY DINNER	• Campfire Cassoulet (page 42) • Toffee Apple Crepes (page 54) 🏠
SUNDAY BREAKFAST	• Ricotta & Strawberry Croissants (page 30)
SUNDAY LUNCH	• Tonno e Fagioli (page 38) 🏠

SHOPPING LIST

Spices & Flavorings
bay leaf (1)
chili flakes, dried (1 tsp.)
mustard, Dijon (1 jar)
olive oil (1 bottle)
salt & pepper
soy sauce (¼ cup)
sugar, any variety
  (⅔ cup)
sunflower oil (2 tbsp.)
Vinaigrette (¼ cup),
  (page 21)
wine, red (½ cup)

Cans & Jars
beans, cannellini or navy
  (3 lb. 12 oz.)
peanut butter (1 jar)

plum tomatoes, whole
  (1 lb. 12 oz.)
strawberry jam (1 jar)
tuna (9 oz.)

Dry Foods
bread (1 sliced loaf)
Camping Crepes (4),
  (page 171)
ciabatta rolls (4)
croissants (4)

Meat
bacon (8 slices)
bacon, thick-cut
  (8 oz.)
chicken breast filets (4)
pork loin steaks (4)
sausages, Toulouse (8)

Chilled Foods
butter (2¼ sticks)
crème fraîche (1¼ cups)
eggs, extra large (3)
ricotta cheese (½ cup)

Fruit & Vegetables
apples (4)
bean sprouts (4 cups)
carrots (2)
cucumber, small (1)
garlic cloves (6)
lime (1)
onions (2)
pineapple (1)
radishes (14–15)
thyme sprig (1)
tomato, large (1)

🍴 Meal Plan for Vegetarians

FRIDAY DINNER	• Tomatoes & Chickpeas with Couscous (page 50) • Toffee Apple Crepes (page 54) 🏠
SATURDAY BREAKFAST	• Ricotta & Strawberry Croissants (page 30)
SATURDAY LUNCH	• Spanish Tortilla (page 39)
SATURDAY DINNER	• Cashew Stir-Fry (page 51) • Prune & Orange Yogurt (page 56)
SUNDAY BREAKFAST	• Grandpa's Eggs (page 33)
SUNDAY LUNCH	• Chinese Noodle Soup (page 36)

SHOPPING LIST

Spices & Flavorings
chili sauce (1 bottle)
olive oil (1 bottle)
salt & pepper
soy sauce (1 bottle)
sugar, any variety (¼ cup)
sunflower oil (2 tbsp.)
vegetable bouillon cubes
  (2)

Cans & Jars
chickpeas (1 lb. 13 oz.)
diced tomatoes
  (1 lb. 12 oz.)
strawberry jam (1 jar)

Dry Foods
bread, crusty (½ loaf)
Camping Crepes (4),
  (page 171)
cashews (1½ cups)
couscous (2¼ cups)
croissants (4)
prunes, pitted (2 cups)

Chilled Foods
butter (2¼ sticks)
eggs, extra large (8)
noodles, fresh (1 lb. 10 oz.)
orange juice (1¼ cups)
ricotta cheese (½ cup)
yogurt, thick natural
  (3½ cups)

Fruit & Vegetables
apples (4)
bok choy (4)
broccoli, head (1)
garlic cloves (2)
ginger root (2-in. piece)
mint leaves (2 handfuls)
mushrooms (9 oz.)
new potatoes (1 lb. 2 oz.)
onions (2)
scallions (4)

Oatmeal with Bananas & Honey

SERVES: 4
PREPARATION TIME: 5 MINUTES
COOKING TIME: ABOUT 10 MINUTES

heaped 1½ cups rolled
  oats

generous 1½ cups milk
a pinch of salt

4 bananas
¼–½ cup honey, to serve

1 Put the oats, milk, salt and generous 1½ cups water in a saucepan. Bring to a boil over medium heat. Put the saucepan over low heat and cook about 4 to 5 minutes, stirring occasionally, until all the liquid has been absorbed and the oats are swollen and soft. Peel and slice the bananas.
2 Divide the oatmeal into bowls and top each with a sliced banana. Serve hot, drizzled with 1 to 2 tablespoons of honey, to taste.

Ricotta & Strawberry Croissants

SERVES: 4
PREPARATION TIME: 5 MINUTES
COOKING TIME: ABOUT 3 MINUTES

½ cup ricotta cheese

8 teaspoons strawberry
  jam

4 croissants, split
  lengthwise

1 Spoon 2 tablespoons of the ricotta cheese and 2 teaspoons of the jam over each croissant base, then cover with the top halves of the croissants.
2 Cook the croissants over low heat on a portable barbecue or in a grill pan about 2 to 3 minutes, turning once, until the outsides are crisp but not browned. Serve hot.

Eggy Bread with Bacon & Tomatoes

SERVES: 4
PREPARATION TIME: 5 MINUTES
COOKING TIME: ABOUT 15 MINUTES

heaped 1¾ cups canned
   whole plum tomatoes
1 tablespoon butter or
   sunflower oil, plus extra
   for frying if needed

8 bacon slices
3 extra large eggs, beaten
4 slices of bread
salt and pepper

mustard, any variety or
   barbecue sauce, to serve

1 Put the canned tomatoes in a saucepan, season with salt and pepper, then bring to a boil over high heat. Put the saucepan over medium heat and simmer about 10 minutes until the sauce is fairly thick.

2 Meanwhile, heat the butter in a skillet over medium heat, then add the bacon and fry until crisp. Remove the bacon from the pan and wrap in tinfoil to keep it warm, leaving the fat in the pan. Put the skillet over low heat to keep it hot.

3 Put the eggs in a bowl and season with salt and pepper. Dip the slices of bread into the egg mixture, turning to coat on both sides, until the bread absorbs some of the mixture. Put the skillet over medium heat. Working in batches if necessary, cook the eggy bread about 2 minutes on each side until starting to crisp, adding more butter to the pan as needed.

4 Serve immediately with the tomatoes, bacon slices and mustard.

Grandpa's Eggs

This simple recipe is a firm favorite with our kids. We call it "Grandpa's Eggs" because this is how Grandpa used to make them. As a variation, try it sprinkled with chopped ham or crispy bacon.

SERVES: 4
PREPARATION TIME: 5 MINUTES
COOKING TIME: ABOUT 4 MINUTES

4 extra large eggs   salt and pepper
½ loaf of crusty bread, torn
   into pieces and buttered

1 Bring a saucepan of water to a simmer and add the eggs, then put the saucepan over medium heat and cook about 3 to 4 minutes. Remove the eggs from the pan and plunge them into cold water to stop them from cooking any further. Transfer to a bowl and set aside until cool enough to handle.

2 Divide the buttered bread into bowls. Peel the soft-boiled eggs and put one in each bowl, letting the yolks ooze over the bread. If the eggs are still too hot to peel, simply crack them open and scoop the whites and yolks out of the shells. Season with salt and pepper and serve immediately.

Lomo a la Plancha

This is a Spanish classic, and the tomato, olive oil and garlic combination is a great summery alternative to butter or mayonnaise. Wild arugula adds a lovely, peppery touch, so a bit of foraging pays off enormously. Flattening the pork helps you get maximum crispiness combined with succulence.

SERVES: 4
PREPARATION TIME: 10 MINUTES
COOKING TIME: ABOUT 6 MINUTES

4 pork loin steaks or boneless pork chops

4 ciabatta rolls, cut in half horizontally or 2 baguettes, each cut in half horizontally then cut in half lengthwise

1 garlic clove, peeled and halved

1 large tomato, cut in half horizontally

olive oil, for drizzling

salt and pepper

wild arugula, to serve (optional)

1 Put the pork steaks in a large plastic freezer bag. Using a camping mallet, flatten each one until very thin and doubled in size. Pat dry with paper towels and season both sides with salt and pepper.

2 Toast the cut side of the rolls over medium heat on a portable barbecue or in a grill pan until lightly golden. Remove from the heat and set aside.

3 Cook the pork steaks over medium-high heat on a portable barbecue or in a skillet about 2 to 3 minutes on each side until charred and crispy on the outside and juicy on the inside.

4 Meanwhile, rub the garlic onto the toasted side of the rolls. Add a good squeeze of tomato juice and drizzle with a little oil. Put a cooked pork steak on the bottom half of each roll and top with wild arugula, if you can find some. Cover with the top halves of the rolls and serve hot.

Chinese Noodle Soup

If you're looking for a really quick meal to prepare that's both delicious and hugely satisfying, look no further. This soup is just as good without the shrimp, and if you can find a Chinese chili sauce to serve it with, it'll definitely go down a treat!

SERVES: 4
PREPARATION TIME: 10 MINUTES
COOKING TIME: ABOUT 5 MINUTES

4⅓ cups vegetable stock
10½ ounces fresh or dried noodles, such as rice, egg or buckwheat
4 bok choy, stems sliced and leaves left whole or 1 broccoli head, cut into florets

9 ounces mushrooms, thinly sliced
7 ounces cooked jumbo shrimp or raw jumbo shrimp, peeled and deveined (optional)
soy sauce, to taste
chili sauce, to serve

1 Pour the stock into a large saucepan and bring to a boil over high heat.
2 Add the noodles, bok choy and mushrooms and return to a boil. Add the shrimp, if using, and cook 2 to 3 minutes longer until the noodles are cooked, the vegetables are tender and the shrimp are hot. (If you are using raw shrimp, cook about 2 to 3 minutes until the shrimp are pink and completely cooked through.)
3 Remove from the heat and add a little soy sauce, to taste. Divide into bowls and serve hot with chili sauce.

Tonno e Fagioli

This is a simplified version of the classic Italian tuna and white bean salad.

SERVES: 4
PREPARATION TIME: 5 MINUTES

9 ounces canned tuna, drained

1 pound 13 ounces canned cannellini beans, drained

7 ounces radishes, finely sliced

¼ cup Vinaigrette (page 21)

sliced bread or crusty bread, to serve

1 Put the tuna, cannellini beans and radishes in a large bowl. Sprinkle the vinaigrette over the top and toss to combine. Serve with sliced bread.

Prepare ahead: Make the Vinaigrette (page 21) at home before you leave.

Sardine Pâté

SERVES: 4
PREPARATION TIME: 5 MINUTES

4¼ ounces canned sardine fillets, drained

7 ounces cream cheese

juice of ½ lemon

salt and pepper

4 pita breads, to serve

2 carrots, peeled and cut into sticks, to serve

1 cucumber, cut into sticks, to serve

1 Put the sardines in a bowl and mash well with a fork to form a coarse paste. Stir in the cream cheese and lemon juice, then season to taste with salt and pepper. Serve with pita breads, carrot sticks and cucumber sticks.

Spanish Tortilla

This deep omelet is the classic Spanish "meal in one pan."

SERVES: 4
PREPARATION TIME: 15 MINUTES
COOKING TIME: ABOUT 50 MINUTES

6 tablespoons olive oil or sunflower oil

2 onions, finely sliced

1 pound 2 ounces new potatoes, halved lengthwise and thinly sliced

4 extra large eggs, beaten

salt and pepper

1 Heat 2 tablespoons of the oil in a large skillet over low heat. Add the onions and a pinch of salt and give them a good stir to prevent them sticking to the bottom of the pan. Cook, stirring, at least 15 minutes until the onions are soft and golden. Remove the pan from the heat and push the onions to the side of the pan. Tilting the pan, squeeze the onions, using the back of a wooden spoon, to remove any excess oil. Transfer the onions to a large bowl and set aside, leaving the oil in the pan.

2 Put the skillet over medium heat and add another 2 tablespoons of the oil. Add the potatoes and cook about 15 to 20 minutes until tender but make sure they don't crisp up too much.

3 Add the eggs and potatoes to the onion mixture, season with salt and pepper and mix.

4 Put the skillet over high heat and add the remaining oil. When the oil starts to smoke, pour in the egg mixture, evenly spreading out the ingredients with a wooden spoon. Cook over low heat about 5 minutes until the tortilla turns golden brown on the bottom. Remove the pan from the heat and turn the tortilla out onto a plate. Slide the tortilla back into the pan, runny-side down, and cook over low heat 5 minutes longer until golden brown and set. Cut into wedges and serve hot, straight from the pan.

Lebanese Kebabs with Chickpea Salad

SERVES: 4
PREPARATION TIME: 20 MINUTES, PLUS AT LEAST 1 HOUR MARINATING
COOKING TIME: ABOUT 10 MINUTES

1 pound 5 ounces boneless lamb leg or shoulder, trimmed of fat and cut into bite-size pieces
salt and pepper
warm pita breads, to serve

MARINADE:
juice of 1 lemon
1 garlic clove, crushed
½ teaspoon ground allspice

GARLIC DIP:
juice of ½ lemon
½ garlic clove, crushed
¼ cup thick plain yogurt
2 tablespoons olive oil

CHICKPEA SALAD:
2 tomatoes, finely chopped
½ cucumber, finely chopped
14½ ounces canned chickpeas, drained
2 handfuls of parsley leaves, finely chopped
juice of ½ lemon
1 tablespoon olive oil

1 If using wooden skewers, soak them in cold water at least 30 minutes before grilling. To make the marinade, put all of the ingredients in a plastic freezer bag. Season with salt and pepper, then add the lamb and seal the bag. Rub the marinade all over the lamb and let marinate in a cooler at least 1 hour, preferably overnight.

2 To make the dip, mix all of the ingredients together in a bowl and season with salt and pepper. Cover and set aside.

3 To make the salad, put all of the ingredients in a large bowl. Season with salt and pepper and toss gently but thoroughly.

4 Thread the lamb onto skewers. Cook, turning frequently, over high heat on a portable barbecue or in a grill pan about 8 minutes until browned and crispy on the outside but pink in the middle. Remove the lamb from the skewers and serve in warm pita breads with the garlic dip and the chickpea salad.

 Prepare ahead: Take the lamb in the marinade if you're planning to eat it on the first night.

Campfire Cassoulet

For an authentic touch, fry some breadcrumbs in oil or butter and sprinkle them over the top of the cassoulet before you serve it.

SERVES: 4
PREPARATION TIME: 10 MINUTES
COOKING TIME: ABOUT 1¼ HOURS

8 Toulouse sausages, quartered
8 ounces thick-cut bacon or pancetta, cubed
1 tablespoon olive oil or butter
2 onions, finely sliced
4 garlic cloves, chopped

1 thyme sprig or 1 teaspoon dried thyme
1 bay leaf
½ cup red wine
heaped 1¾ cups canned whole plum tomatoes or canned diced tomatoes

1 pound 13 ounces canned cannellini or navy beans, drained
salt and pepper
Dijon mustard, to serve

1 Put the sausages in a large skillet or saucepan over high heat. Cook about 5 minutes until browned, then add the bacon and cook 5 minutes longer. Push the sausages and bacon to the side of the pan. Alternatively, transfer them to a plate and set aside, leaving the fat in the pan.

2 Add the oil to the pan, then add the onions and cook about 5 minutes until translucent and softened. Add the garlic and herbs and cook 1 minute longer.

3 Add the wine and bring to a boil, then add the canned tomatoes and season with salt and pepper. Return the browned sausages and bacon to the pan, if necessary. Put the pan over low heat and simmer, partially covered, about 30 to 45 minutes. Add the cannellini beans and cook about 15 minutes until the cassoulet has thickened. Serve hot with mustard.

Tuscan Ham, Spinach & Cannellini Stew

This is our camping version of a dish we regularly prepare at home—often in huge quantities. At home we would cook our own ham and soak our own beans, but to save on cooking times and fuel we've come up with this quick and easy recipe. It's foolproof to prepare and just as good!

SERVES: 4
PREPARATION TIME: 10 MINUTES
COOKING TIME: ABOUT 25 MINUTES

2 tablespoons olive oil
1 large onion, chopped
2 garlic cloves, finely chopped
9 ounces boneless, cooked smoked ham, cut into bite-size pieces

14½ ounces canned cannellini beans, drained
4⅓ cups ham or vegetable stock
9 ounces fresh or defrosted, frozen spinach
pepper

Parmesan cheese, grated, to serve

1 Heat the oil in a large saucepan over medium heat. Add the onion and cook about 10 minutes until softened. Add the garlic and ham and cook, stirring continuously, about 1 minute.

2 Add the cannellini beans and stock and bring to a boil. Put the pan over low heat and simmer gently, stirring occasionally, about 10 minutes. Season to taste with pepper.

3 Put the pan over medium heat, then add the spinach and return to a boil. Remove from the heat and let cool slightly. Serve hot sprinkled with Parmesan.

Chicken, Tomato & Rosemary Packages

SERVES: 4
PREPARATION TIME: 10 MINUTES
COOKING TIME: ABOUT 30 MINUTES

1 pound 11 ounces new
   potatoes, scrubbed and
   quartered
6 tablespoons olive oil
4 tomatoes, each cut into
   4 thick slices

4 boneless, skinless
   chicken breast filets or
   8 boneless, skinless
   chicken thigh filets
juice of 1 lemon

2 garlic cloves, crushed
4 small rosemary sprigs
salt and pepper

1 Put the potatoes on a piece of tinfoil large enough to make a package. Drizzle with 2 tablespoons of the oil and season with salt and pepper. Pull up the tinfoil to enclose, tightly sealing the seams of the package to prevent it from leaking. Cook in the glowing embers of a portable charcoal barbecue or open fire about 30 minutes. Remember to move the package from time to time to let the potatoes cook evenly. Alternatively, cook the potatoes in plenty of salted boiling water about 10 minutes until soft. Remove from the heat, then drain and return to the pan. Add 2 tablespoons of the oil, season with salt and pepper and roughly mash with a fork.

2 Meanwhile, cut four rectangles of tinfoil, each large enough to enclose a chicken breast. Arrange 4 tomato slices in the middle of each rectangle, top with a chicken breast and season with salt and pepper. Scrunch up the edges of each rectangle, then sprinkle one-quarter of the lemon juice, garlic and the remaining oil over each chicken breast and top each with a rosemary sprig.

3 Pull up the tinfoil to enclose, tightly sealing the seams of the packages to prevent them from leaking. Cook in the glowing embers of a portable charcoal barbecue or open fire about 20 minutes until the juices run clear when the thickest part of the meat is pierced with the tip of a sharp knife or skewer. Remember to move the packages from time to time to let the chicken cook evenly. Alternatively, cook over high heat in a grill pan, about 8 minutes on each side. Serve hot with the foil-roasted or fork-mashed potatoes.

Chicken Satay Skewers & Asian Salad

SERVES: 4
PREPARATION TIME: 15 MINUTES
COOKING TIME: ABOUT 20 MINUTES

4 boneless, skinless
   chicken breast filets,
   cut into bite-size pieces

SATAY SAUCE & DRESSING:
juice of 1 lime
1 garlic clove, crushed
2 tablespoons sunflower oil
¼ cup soy sauce
2 tablespoons sugar, any
   variety or honey
a pinch of dried chili flakes
½ cup peanut butter

ASIAN SALAD:
2 carrots, cut into
   matchsticks
1 small cucumber, cut into
   matchsticks
4 cups bean sprouts

1 If using wooden skewers, soak them in cold water at least 30 minutes before grilling. To make the sauce and dressing, put the lime juice, garlic, oil, soy sauce, sugar and chili flakes in a cup and mix well. Reserve half of the mixture for the salad dressing and pour the other half into a saucepan for the sauce.

2 Put the saucepan over low heat and add the peanut butter. Gently bring to a simmer, stirring occasionally, about 5 minutes until thickened. Add a little water if the sauce becomes too thick to pour. Remove from the heat. Reserve half of the sauce in a bowl, for dipping, leaving the remaining sauce in the pan.

3 To make the salad, mix together the carrots, cucumber and bean sprouts in a large bowl. Add the salad dressing and toss well.

4 Thread the chicken onto skewers. Cook over medium heat on a portable barbecue or in a grill pan 1 minute, turning once, then brush with some of the remaining sauce. Cook, turning and brushing with sauce, about 4 to 6 minutes, until the juices run clear.

5 Serve immediately with the reserved satay sauce and with the salad.

Soy & Ginger Salmon Packages

We love this served with noodles and Chinese chili sauce. If you can cook the salmon in the embers of an open fire, you'll get an added charred dimension. You could also serve it with the Cashew Stir-Fry (page 51).

SERVES: 4
PREPARATION TIME: 10 MINUTES
COOKING TIME: ABOUT 10 MINUTES

4 teaspoons sunflower oil
4 salmon steaks or 4 boneless, skinless salmon fillets
¼ cup soy sauce, plus extra to serve

1-inch piece of ginger root, peeled and finely chopped
4 bok choy, stems sliced and leaves left whole or 1 broccoli head, cut into florets

cooked noodles or rice, to serve
lime wedges, to serve
chili sauce, to serve

1 Cut four rectangles of tinfoil, each large enough to enclose a salmon steak. Scrunch up the edges of each rectangle, then spoon 1 teaspoon of the oil into each one and top with a salmon steak.

2 Sprinkle each salmon steak with 1 tablespoon of the soy sauce and one-quarter of the ginger. Pull up the tinfoil to enclose, tightly sealing the seams of the salmon packages to prevent them from leaking.

3 Cook over low heat on a portable barbecue or in a grill pan about 10 minutes until the salmon is opaque and just cooked. For a real taste of the outdoors, cook the packages in the glowing embers of an open fire. Remember to move the packages from time to time to let the salmon steaks cook evenly.

4 Meanwhile, bring a saucepan of lightly salted water to a boil and add the bok choy. Blanch about 3 to 5 minutes until the bok choy is tender but still retains a slight crunch. Unwrap the salmon packages and serve hot with the blanched bok choy, noodles, lime wedges, soy sauce and chili sauce.

Tomatoes & Chickpeas with Couscous

The mint in this dish transforms humble ingredients into something delicious with Moroccan-inspired flavors. It's one of our favorite camping dishes and the children absolutely love it.

SERVES: 4
PREPARATION TIME: 5 MINUTES
COOKING TIME: ABOUT 12 MINUTES

3¼ cups canned diced tomatoes

heaped 2 cups couscous

1 pound 13 ounces canned chickpeas, drained

2 handfuls of mint leaves, coarsely chopped

1 tablespoon olive oil

salt and pepper

1 Pour scant 2½ cups water into a large saucepan and bring to a boil over high heat.

2 Put the canned tomatoes in a large skillet and simmer over medium heat about 10 minutes until the juices have thickened. Season with salt and pepper.

3 Meanwhile, put the couscous in a large bowl or plastic container and pour the boiled water over the top. Season with salt and pepper and cover with a lid. Let soak at least 5 minutes until the grains are tender.

4 Add the chickpeas to the tomatoes and cook about 2 minutes until warmed through, then stir in the mint leaves. Fluff up the couscous with a fork, add the oil and mix well. Spoon the couscous onto plates and serve hot, topped with the tomatoes, chickpeas and mint leaves.

Cashew Stir-Fry

Stir-fries are always fantastic first-night meals as they are quick and easy to prepare in one pan. This one is no exception. The broccoli in the recipe can be substituted with green beans or any combination of mixed vegetables.

SERVES: 4
PREPARATION TIME: 5 MINUTES
COOKING TIME: ABOUT 10 MINUTES

2 tablespoons sunflower oil
1 broccoli head, cut into
   small florets
2 garlic cloves, finely
   chopped
2-inch piece of ginger
   root, peeled and finely
   chopped

4 scallions, sliced
1 tablespoon soy sauce,
   plus extra to taste
heaped 1⅓ cups cashews
1 pound fresh noodles
chili sauce, to serve

1 Heat the oil in a large skillet over high heat. Add the broccoli and stir-fry, stirring frequently, 1 minute.

2 Add the garlic, ginger, scallions, soy sauce and ¼ cup water and stir-fry 3 minutes longer until the broccoli is just tender, adding a little more water if needed. Add the cashews and stir-fry 1 minute longer.

3 Add the noodles and stir-fry about 2 to 3 minutes until the noodles are cooked. Taste and add more soy sauce, if you like. Serve immediately with chili sauce.

Barbecued Pineapple Wedges

Put this on the portable barbecue to cook just before you sit down to eat your dinner. The longer it has to cook, the more caramelized your pineapple will become. For an extra dimension, add a splash of rum to the butter.

SERVES: 4
PREPARATION TIME: 15 MINUTES
COOKING TIME: ABOUT 25 MINUTES

1 pineapple
¼ cup (½ stick) butter

2 tablespoons sugar, any
variety

1 If using wooden skewers, soak them in cold water at least 30 minutes before grilling.
2 Using a sharp knife, cut the pineapple, including the green top, into quarters lengthwise. Cut between the flesh and the skin to release the flesh, but keep the skin in place. Slice the flesh on each pineapple quarter into chunks and push a long skewer lengthwise through each wedge and into the skin to hold the flesh in place during cooking.
3 Heat the butter in a saucepan over low heat until melted. Remove from the heat, add the sugar and mix. Brush the butter mixture over the pineapple quarters.
4 Cook, skin-side down, over high heat on a portable barbecue or in a grill pan about 20 minutes until golden brown and soft. Serve warm.

Toffee Apple Crepes

SERVES: 4
PREPARATION TIME: 5 MINUTES
COOKING TIME: ABOUT 15 MINUTES

¼ cup (½ stick) butter, plus extra for frying
¼ cup sugar, any variety
4 apples, peeled and each cut into thin wedges

4 Camping Crepes (page 171) or 4 ready-made crepes
crème fraîche, thick plain yogurt or cream, to serve

1 Put the butter and sugar in a skillet over medium-low heat. Cook, stirring, until the butter has melted and the sugar has dissolved. Add the apple wedges and cook about 7 minutes until the apples are soft and the butter mixture starts to turn golden. Transfer the caramelized apples to a bowl and set aside.

2 Return the pan to the heat. Add 1 tablespoon of butter and heat until melted, making sure it covers the bottom of the skillet. Slide 1 of the crepes into the pan and cook about 30 seconds until heated through. Top with one-quarter of the toffee apple mixture, then using a spatula, fold the crepe in half to enclose the filling and transfer to a plate. Repeat with the remaining crepes and filling, adding more butter to the pan if needed. Serve immediately with crème fraîche.

 Prepare ahead: Make up a batch of Camping Crepes (page 171) at home before you leave. Leave to cool completely, then stack between sheets of parchment paper, wrap in tinfoil and store in a sealed plastic freezer bag in a cooler up to 3 days.

Banana, Chocolate & Marshmallow Boats

SERVES: 4
PREPARATION TIME: 2 MINUTES
COOKING TIME: ABOUT 10 MINUTES

4 bananas
8 marshmallows

3½ ounces milk chocolate,
 broken into squares

1 Using a sharp knife, cut a lengthwise slit through the skin of each banana and stuff 2 marshmallows into each slit. Cook the bananas, slit-side up, over medium heat on a portable barbecue or in a grill pan about 10 minutes until the skins have browned.

2 Transfer the bananas to a plate and stuff 3 squares of chocolate into each slit. Serve and watch the chocolate melt before eating.

Prune & Orange Yogurt

SERVES: 4
PREPARATION TIME: 5 MINUTES
COOKING TIME: ABOUT 10 MINUTES

heaped 1½ cups pitted
 prunes, chopped

generous 1 cup orange
 juice

heaped 2 cups thick plain
 yogurt

1 Mix together the prunes and orange juice in a saucepan and simmer over low heat about 7 minutes until the liquid has reduced by half. Remove from the heat and let cool 5 minutes.

2 Beat the prune mixture with a fork to form a coarse puree. Transfer the mixture to a bowl and spoon in the yogurt. Mix thoroughly and serve.

Foil Fruit Cobbler

These are like individual fruit crumbles, cooked in tinfoil. Kids usually like making desserts so this is a good one for them to get involved with.

SERVES: 4
PREPARATION TIME: 15 MINUTES
COOKING TIME: ABOUT 15 MINUTES

5½ tablespoons (¾ stick) butter
heaped 1½ cups rolled oats
½ cup brown sugar

3 apples, pears or large peaches, cut into chunks
thick plain yogurt, cream or pudding, to serve

1 Melt the butter in a saucepan over low heat and stir in the oats and two-thirds of the brown sugar. Remove from the heat and set aside. Put the apples and the remaining brown sugar in a bowl and toss gently but thoroughly.

2 Cut four large squares of tinfoil, each about 12 inches square. Scrunch up the edges of each square and spoon one-quarter of the oat mixture and one-quarter of the apple mixture into each one. Pull up the tinfoil to enclose, tightly sealing the seams of the cobbler packages to prevent them from leaking.

3 Cook, oat-side down, over medium heat on a portable barbecue or in a grill pan about 10 minutes. Remember to move the packages from time to time to let the cobbler packages cook evenly.

4 Turn over the packages and cook 5 minutes longer, then remove them from the heat and let cool 5 minutes. Serve warm straight out of the packages, plain or with yogurt.

BY THE BEACH

By the Beach

Camping near the sea is hard to beat, with long days on the beach followed by leisurely evenings with a barbecue, a light sea breeze and the setting sun. As you would expect, this chapter has a variety of fish dishes as well as other recipes bursting with the taste of the seaside.

Fishing is an integral part of coastal life from India to the Caribbean to the Mediterranean and eating freshly caught seafood cooked on a portable barbecue is truly great. The Grilled Fish & Smoky Eggplant Salad (page 84) is a favorite with parents and older children, and the Paella (page 87) is our eight-year-old daughter's top camping recipe.

This chapter is also a celebration of all things fresh, sunny and sweet. From Chapatis with Fruit Salad & Honey (page 66) to Fruit Kebabs with Mint & Black Pepper Syrup (page 90)—all made with fresh fruit and locally picked herbs—there are plenty of opportunities to cook up some delicious breakfasts and desserts.

Pack up the key ingredients below and you'll be able to transform any fresh food that you buy (or catch) into a feast fit for your surroundings. You could also use the meal plans to guide you through some of our favorite beach-side recipes.

KEY INGREDIENTS

- chilies
- cumin, ground
- garam masala
- garlic
- harissa paste
- herbs, fresh (cilantro leaves, mint leaves, parsley leaves and rosemary sprigs)
- lemons
- maple syrup and/or light corn syrup
- olive oil
- oregano, dried
- saffron
- salt and pepper
- smoked paprika
- sugar and/or honey
- Vinaigrette (page 21)

TIPS

Butterflying a leg of lamb

The Mediterranean Butterflied Lamb with Foil-Roasted Vegetable Couscous (page 78) is a great dinner to share on the beach as the sun sets. "Butterflying" opens out the meat so it can be grilled quickly and evenly, making it deliciously crisp on the outside and succulent and juicy on the inside. If you can't find a butcher to do it for you, do it yourself by following these easy steps:

1 Trim the skin and excess fat from the lamb leg and cut out the bone.
2 Make a cut along each side of the bone channel along the grain of the meat, cutting halfway down through the flesh. Open out the meat and turn it over.
3 Make 3 horizontal cuts into the flesh midway between the cuts on the other side and open out the meat like a fan. Make more cuts if necessary with the aim of opening out the lamb to an even thickness of about 1 inch. Don't worry if it doesn't stay in one piece, it will still cook beautifully.

Gutting a fish

Nothing compares to the taste of freshly caught fish. When you cook them whole over a flame the scales will crisp up nicely so there's no need for descaling. However, you will need to scale the fish if you're cooking them in a grill pan. Simply run the back of a knife along the fish from back to front, against the grain, and the scales should come off quite easily. You'll always need to gut your fish, so follow these steps:

1 Using a sharp knife, slice open the belly of the fish from head to tail-end.
2 Gently pull out the guts and thoroughly rinse the belly cavity.
3 Using a blunt knife, scrape along the top of the belly cavity to make sure all the guts have been removed. Rinse thoroughly, then pat dry with paper towels.

🍴 Meal Plan for Young Kids

FRIDAY DINNER	• Grilled Pork Chops with German Potato Salad (page 81) 🏠 • S'mores (page 94)
SATURDAY BREAKFAST	• Breakfast Quesadillas (page 70)
SATURDAY LUNCH	• One-Pot Salade Niçoise (page 75) 🏠
SATURDAY DINNER	• Paella (page 87) • Campsite Mess (page 94)
SUNDAY BREAKFAST	• Blueberry Pancakes with Maple Syrup (page 69) 🏠
SUNDAY LUNCH	• Chakchouka (page 77)

SHOPPING LIST

Spices & Flavorings
balsamic vinegar (2 tsp.)
chicken bouillon cubes (2)
maple syrup (1 bottle)
mayonnaise (1 jar)
mustard, Dijon (1 jar)
olive oil (1 bottle)
saffron (a pinch)
salt & pepper
smoked paprika (1 tsp.)
sugar, granulated (1½ tbsp.)
Vinaigrette (3 tbsp.),
    (page 21)

Cans & Jars
anchovy fillets (1 tin)
harissa paste (1 jar)
olives, black pitted (½ cup)
pickles, large (4)
tuna (9 oz.)

Dry Foods
baking powder (4 tsp.)
chocolate, any variety
    (3½ oz.)
flour, self-rising (2 cups)
graham crackers (1 packet)
marshmallows (1 bag)
meringues, ready-made (4)
paella rice (2¼ cups)
pita breads (4)
soft flour tortillas, small (8)

Meat & Fish
chorizo (7 oz.)
ham (4 slices)
pork chops (4)
shrimp, raw jumbo (7 oz.)

Chilled Foods
butter (2¼ sticks)
crème fraîche (1¼ cups)
eggs, extra large (14)
milk (1 pint)

Fruit & Vegetables
beans, green (1½ cups)
bell peppers, red (4)
blueberries (1½ cups)
garlic cloves (5)
lemon (1)
lettuce, large crunchy head (1)
onions, red (2)
new potatoes (2 lb. 10 oz.)
parsley leaves (1 handful)
peas, frozen (1¼ cups)
scallions (6)
strawberries (2½ cups)
tomatoes, large (2)

🍴 Meal Plan for Older Kids

FRIDAY DINNER	• Mediterranean Butterflied Lamb with Foil-Roasted Vegetable Couscous (page 78) • Mango & Passion Fruit Fool (page 93)
SATURDAY BREAKFAST	• Smoked Salmon & Scrambled Eggs (page 71)
SATURDAY LUNCH	• Barbecued Steak & Tomato Salad (page 72) 🏠
SATURDAY DINNER	• Grilled Fish & Smoky Eggplant Salad (page 84) • Fruit Kebabs with Mint & Black Pepper Syrup (page 90)
SUNDAY BREAKFAST	• Chapatis with Fruit Salad & Honey (page 66)
SUNDAY LUNCH	• Chakchouka (page 77)

SHOPPING LIST

Spices & Flavorings
cumin, ground (4 tsp.)
honey (1 bottle)
olive oil (1 bottle)
salt & pepper
smoked paprika (4 tsp.)
sugar, any variety (⅓ cup)

Cans & Jars
harissa paste (1 jar)

Dry Foods
bread, crusty (1 loaf)
couscous (1¼ cups)
crusty rolls (4)
flour, chapati (1¼ cups)
pita breads (4)

Meat & Fish
fish, sea bream, sea bass
  or mullet (4 whole)
lamb, butterflied leg (1)
smoked salmon (4 slices)
steak, thick-cut tenderloin (2)

Chilled Foods
butter (2¼ sticks)
eggs, extra large (12)
yogurt, thick plain
  (2 cups)

Fruit & Vegetables
bananas (4)
bell peppers, red (5)
butternut squash (1)
cherry tomatoes (1 lb. 5 oz.)
chilies (2)
eggplants, large (2)
garlic cloves (11)
kiwis (4)
lemons (3)
mangoes (4)
mint leaves (1 handful)
onions, red (4)
parsley leaves (3 handfuls)
passion fruit (4)
pineapple, small (1)
tomatoes, large (2)

🍴 Meal Plan for Vegetarians

FRIDAY DINNER	• Tofu Kebabs with Paprika Dressing (page 82) • Fruit Kebabs with Mint & Black Pepper Syrup (page 90)
SATURDAY BREAKFAST	• Chapatis with Fruit Salad & Honey (page 66)
SATURDAY LUNCH	• Spinach, Tomato & Garlic Soup (page 76)
SATURDAY DINNER	• Butternut Squash Tagine with Nut & Raisin Couscous (page 89) • Sticky Toffee Bananas (page 95)
SUNDAY BREAKFAST	• Blueberry Pancakes with Maple Syrup (page 69) 🏠
SUNDAY LUNCH	• Watermelon & Feta Salad (page 76)

BY THE BEACH

SHOPPING LIST

Spices & Flavorings
garam masala (1 tsp.)
honey (1 bottle)
maple syrup (1 bottle)
olive oil (1 bottle)
salt & pepper
smoked paprika (1 tsp.)
sugar, granulated (⅓ cup)
vegetable bouillon cubes (2)

Cans & Jars
diced tomatoes
   (1 lb. 12 oz.)
harissa paste (1 jar)

Dry Foods
baking powder (4 tsp.)
bread, crusty (1 loaf)
couscous (2⅓ cups)
flour, chapati (1¼ cups)
flour, self-rising (2 cups)
pita breads (4)
raisin & nut mix (½ cup)

Chilled Foods
butter (2¼ sticks)
crème fraîche (1¼ cups)
eggs, extra large (2)
feta cheese (7 oz.)
milk (1 pint)
orange juice (2 tbsp.)
tofu (14 oz.)

Fruit & Vegetables
bananas (8)
bell pepper, red (1)
blueberries (1½ cups)
butternut squash, large (1)
cherry tomatoes (20)
cilantro leaves (1 handful)
garlic cloves (8)
kiwis (4)
lemons (2)
mint leaves (3 handfuls)
onion, large (1)
parsley leaves (1 handful)
peaches (2)
pineapple, small (1)
spinach (7–8 cups)
tomatoes (4)
watermelon, small (1)

Chapatis with Fruit Salad & Honey

The longer you knead the chapati dough, the lighter your chapatis will be. Instead of packing a heavy rolling pin, just use a clean, empty glass bottle to roll them out.

SERVES: 4
PREPARATION TIME: 20 MINUTES, PLUS 10 MINUTES RESTING
COOKING TIME: ABOUT 8 MINUTES

heaped 1 cup chapati flour, all-purpose white flour or wholewheat flour, plus extra for dusting
a pinch of salt

1 teaspoon olive oil or sunflower oil
8 ounces fruit, cut into bite-size pieces

2 tablespoons honey
butter, to serve

1 Put the flour and salt in a bowl. Make a well in the center of the mixture and pour in ¼ cup water. Using your hands, mix the ingredients together to make a firm dough, adding a little water if it is too dry. Pour the oil into your hands and rub it over the dough, then knead at least 5 minutes, until smooth. Cover and let rest 10 minutes.

2 Meanwhile, put the fruit in another bowl and drizzle the honey over the top. Toss gently but thoroughly.

3 Heat a skillet over high heat. Divide the dough into 4 equal balls, then flatten each ball and dust with flour. Roll out 1 ball of dough into a circle about 5 inches in diameter to make a chapati. Slide the chapati into the pan and cook about 30 to 60 seconds until bubbles appear on the surface. Using a spatula, flip it over and cook 30 to 60 seconds longer, then flip it over again and press down gently until it puffs up. Transfer to a plate, cover with a clean dish towel and repeat with the remaining balls of dough.

4 Top each chapati with a little butter and one-quarter of the fruit salad. Roll each chapati into a cone shape and serve warm.

Blueberry Pancakes with Maple Syrup

MAKES: 8
PREPARATION TIME: 5 MINUTES, PLUS 10 MINUTES STANDING
COOKING TIME: ABOUT 12 MINUTES

6 tablespoons (¾ stick) butter, plus extra for frying and to serve
scant 2 cups self-rising flour
1 tablespoon granulated sugar
4 teaspoons baking powder
½ teaspoon salt
2 extra large eggs, beaten
generous 1½ cups milk
heaped 1½ cups blueberries
maple syrup, to serve

BY THE BEACH

1 Heat the butter in a saucepan over low heat until melted. Remove from the heat and let cool a little. Mix together the flour, sugar, baking powder and salt in a large plastic bowl.

2 Put the eggs, milk and melted butter in a large pitcher and beat until well mixed. Make a well in the center of the flour mixture and slowly add the egg mixture. Beat slowly with a wooden spoon to draw in the flour to make a smooth batter. Cover and let stand 10 minutes.

3 Heat 1 tablespoon of butter in a skillet over medium heat. Working in batches, pour 2 tablespoons of the batter into one half of the pan to make a pancake and then pour 2 more tablespoons into the other half. As soon as the pancakes start to set, scatter a handful of blueberries over the top of each one. Cook about 1 minute until the underside of the pancakes are golden brown, then flip the pancakes over and cook 1 minute longer. Transfer to a plate and repeat with the remaining batter and blueberries, adding more butter to the pan as needed. Serve warm, drizzled with maple syrup and extra butter, if you like.

Prepare ahead: Combine the dry ingredients at home before you leave. Store the mixture in a large airtight container up to 1 month.

Breakfast Quesadillas

One of the good things about this breakfast—apart from it being a favorite with the kids—is that you don't need plates! You could also add cheese, or replace the ham with cooked bacon. Double the quantities if you're hungry.

SERVES: 4
PREPARATION TIME: 2 MINUTES
COOKING TIME: ABOUT 15 MINUTES

8 small or 4 large soft
   flour tortillas, buttered
4 slices of ham

4 extra large eggs
salt and pepper

1 Heat a skillet over high heat. Put 1 tortilla into the hot pan, butter-side up, and top with 1 slice of ham. (If you're cooking a large tortilla, top one side of the tortilla with ham so you can fold it in half later.)

2 Crack an egg on top of the ham and season with salt and pepper. As soon as the egg white starts to set, either top the filling with another small tortilla, or fold the large tortilla in half to enclose the filling.

3 Cook about 30 seconds, then slide a spatula under the tortilla, flip it over and cook 1 minute on the other side until the egg white has set. Transfer to a plate and repeat with the remaining ingredients to make 3 more quesadillas. Serve hot.

Smoked Salmon & Scrambled Eggs

For this recipe, it's really worth buying some fresh farm eggs if you can. Heat does nothing for smoked salmon, so it spoils it if it is thrown into the pan with the scrambled eggs. Served like this, however, it's delicious.

SERVES: 4
PREPARATION TIME: 5 MINUTES
COOKING TIME: ABOUT 5 MINUTES

¼ cup (½ stick) butter
8 extra large eggs, beaten

4 crusty rolls, each cut in
half horizontally

4 slices of smoked salmon
salt and pepper

1 Heat half of the butter in a saucepan over medium heat and season the eggs with salt and pepper. When the butter starts to froth, pour the eggs into the pan. Cook about 4 to 5 minutes, stirring frequently to prevent the eggs from sticking to the pan. When the eggs are almost set but still slightly runny, remove the pan from the heat as they will continue to cook a little.

2 Spread the remaining butter over the cut sides of each roll. Spoon one-quarter of the scrambled eggs over each roll and top with a slice of smoked salmon. Season with pepper and serve warm.

Barbecued Steak & Tomato Salad

SERVES: 4
PREPARATION TIME: 10 MINUTES, PLUS 10 MINUTES MARINATING
COOKING TIME: ABOUT 8 MINUTES

2 teaspoons smoked
  paprika
3 tablespoons olive oil
2 thick-cut steaks, such as
  tenderloin
2 teaspoons lemon juice or
  Marinade Base (page 21)

1 teaspoon sugar, any
  variety
1 small red onion, finely
  sliced
½ teaspoon salt, plus extra
  for seasoning

14 ounces cherry tomatoes,
  halved
1 handful of parsley leaves,
  finely chopped
crusty bread, to serve

1 Mix together 1 teaspoon of the paprika and 1 tablespoon of the oil in a bowl. Using your hands, rub the mixture over both sides of each steak. Cover and let marinate in a cooler 10 minutes.

2 Meanwhile, in a large bowl, mix together the lemon juice, sugar, onion, salt and the remaining paprika and oil. Let stand 10 minutes to let the onion soften a little and lose its sharpness.

3 Season the steaks with salt and cook over high heat on a portable barbecue or in a grill pan about 3 to 4 minutes on each side. Remove from the heat and let rest, covered, 5 minutes, before slicing into strips.

4 Add the cherry tomatoes, parsley leaves and sliced steak to the onion mixture and toss gently but thoroughly. Check the seasoning and add extra salt if needed. Serve warm or cold with crusty bread.

 Prepare ahead: Make the salad up to 1 day in advance and store in an airtight container in a cooler. If using, make the Marinade Base (page 21) at home before you leave.

One-Pot Salade Niçoise

Some say you shouldn't cook anything in the same pan you boil your eggs in, but we reckon you can break the rules a bit when you're camping! The trick with this one is getting the order right.

SERVES: 4
PREPARATION TIME: 15 MINUTES
COOKING TIME: ABOUT 15 MINUTES

4 new potatoes, quartered or 8 baby new potatoes, halved
4 extra large eggs
7 ounces green beans

1 large crunchy head of lettuce or 2 Little Gem lettuces, roughly torn
9 ounces canned tuna, drained

1¾ ounces jarred or canned anchovy fillets, drained
½ cup pitted black olives, halved
salt and pepper
3 tablespoons Vinaigrette (page 21), to serve

1 Put the potatoes in a large saucepan of salted water. Bring to a boil over high heat and cook about 5 minutes. Add the eggs and beans, then return to a boil and cook 5 minutes longer. Drain all of the ingredients, refresh in cold water and drain again. Return the ingredients to the pan and let cool a little.

2 Put the lettuce in a large bowl and arrange the potatoes, beans and tuna on top.

3 Peel the eggs, cut each one into quarters and add to the salad. Top with the anchovies and season with pepper. Sprinkle the olives over the top and serve drizzled with Vinaigrette.

Prepare ahead: Make the Vinaigrette (page 21) at home before you leave.

Watermelon & Feta Salad

SERVES: 4
PREPARATION TIME: 10 MINUTES

1 small watermelon, cut
  into bite-size pieces
7 ounces feta cheese, diced

2 handfuls of mint leaves,
  finely chopped
2 tablespoons olive oil
pepper

crusty bread, to serve
slices of Parma ham, to
  serve (optional)

1 Put all of the ingredients in a large bowl and toss gently but thoroughly. Season with pepper and serve with crusty bread and slices of Parma ham, if you like.

Spinach, Tomato & Garlic Soup

SERVES: 4
PREPARATION TIME: 10 MINUTES
COOKING TIME: ABOUT 7 MINUTES

1 tablespoon olive oil
6 garlic cloves, finely
  sliced
4 tomatoes, chopped

7–8 cups fresh or
  defrosted, frozen
  spinach, chopped
4⅓ cups vegetable stock

juice of ½ lemon, or
  2 tablespoons Marinade
  Base (page 21)
salt and pepper
crusty bread, to serve

1 Put the oil, garlic and tomatoes in a large saucepan and cook gently over medium heat about 2 to 3 minutes until warmed through. Take care not to overheat the pan or the garlic will sizzle and brown. Add the spinach and season with salt and pepper. Cover with a lid and cook 2 minutes longer.

2 Add the stock and bring to a boil over high heat. Remove from the heat and stir in the lemon juice. Check the seasoning and add extra salt and pepper if needed. Serve hot with crusty bread.

Chakchouka

This very simple Egyptian egg dish makes a delicious lunch or light supper. It's not dissimilar from the Mexican dish, Huevos Rancheros, but in this recipe the eggs are poached rather than fried.

SERVES: 4
PREPARATION TIME: 10 MINUTES
COOKING TIME: ABOUT 25 MINUTES

2 tablespoons olive oil
1 red onion, sliced
2 garlic cloves, sliced
2 red, green or yellow bell peppers, seeded and sliced

2 large tomatoes, diced
½ teaspoon sugar, any variety
1 teaspoon harissa paste or chili sauce (optional)
4 extra large eggs

salt and pepper
pita breads, to serve

1 Heat the oil in a skillet over medium heat. Add the onion and cook about 5 minutes until it starts to soften and turn golden. Add the garlic and cook 1 minute longer, then add the peppers.

2 Cook, stirring occasionally, about 10 minutes until the peppers have softened. Add the tomatoes, sugar and harissa paste, if using. Cook 5 minutes longer, then season with salt and pepper.

3 With the back of a spoon, make 4 deep holes in the mixture and crack an egg into each hole. Season the eggs with salt and pepper. Put the pan over low heat and cover with a lid, tinfoil or a large heatproof plate. Cook about 3 to 4 minutes until the egg whites are cooked through and set, and the yolks are just beginning to firm up. Serve immediately with pita breads.

Mediterranean Butterflied Lamb with Foil-Roasted Vegetable Couscous

SERVES: 4
PREPARATION TIME: 25 MINUTES, PLUS AT LEAST 1 HOUR MARINATING
COOKING TIME: ABOUT 30 MINUTES

BY THE BEACH

juice of 1 lemon
2 garlic cloves, crushed
2 teaspoons smoked
  paprika
2 tablespoons olive oil
1 butterflied leg of lamb
salt and pepper

FOIL-ROASTED VEGETABLE COUSCOUS:
1 pound 2 ounces
  vegetables such as
  squash, onions, peppers
  and leeks, cut into bite-
  size chunks

5 garlic cloves, peeled
  but left whole
¼ cup olive oil
heaped 1 cup couscous
salt and pepper

1 In a large plastic freezer bag, mix together the lemon juice, crushed garlic, paprika and oil. Using your hands, rub the mixture all over the lamb. Cover and let marinate in a cooler at least 1 hour, preferably 3 to 4 hours.

2 Put the vegetables and the whole garlic cloves on a piece of tinfoil large enough to make a package. Drizzle with the oil and season with salt and pepper. Pull up the tinfoil to enclose, tightly sealing the seams of the package to prevent them from leaking. Cook in the embers of a portable charcoal barbecue or open fire about 30 minutes until the vegetables are tender. Remember to move the package from time to time to let the vegetables cook evenly. Alternatively, cook over high heat in a grill pan 8 minutes on each side.

3 Season the lamb with salt and pepper. Cook over high heat on a grill or in a grill pan about 5 to 8 minutes on each side, depending on how pink you like the meat. Remove from the heat, cover and let rest 10 minutes.

4 Meanwhile, put the couscous in a large bowl and pour over 1¼ cups boiled water. Season with salt and pepper and cover. Let soak at least 5 minutes until the grains are tender.

5 Fluff up the couscous with a fork and stir in the roasted vegetables and their juices. Thickly slice the lamb and serve hot with the couscous.

Grilled Pork Chops with German Potato Salad

This is the perfect recipe for the first night of a camping trip as the potato salad can be made at home before you leave. To vary the dish, use horseradish sauce instead of mustard, capers rather than pickles and red onions in place of the scallions.

SERVES: 4
PREPARATION TIME: 5 MINUTES
COOKING TIME: ABOUT 20 MINUTES

4 pork chops
2 teaspoons fresh or dried oregano (optional)
salt and pepper

GERMAN POTATO SALAD:
2 pounds 4 ounces new potatoes, quartered
4 large pickles, diced
6 scallions, finely sliced
3 tablespoons mayonnaise

1 heaped teaspoon Dijon mustard, plus extra to serve
2 tablespoons olive oil
2 teaspoons balsamic vinegar
salt and pepper

1 To make the potato salad, cook the potatoes in plenty of salted boiling water about 10 minutes until tender. Drain and let cool a little.

2 Meanwhile, put the pickles, scallions, mayonnaise, mustard, oil and balsamic vinegar in a large bowl. Mix well and season to taste with salt and pepper. Add the potatoes and toss gently but thoroughly. Cover and set aside.

3 Pat the pork chops dry with paper towels, then season with salt and pepper and sprinkle with oregano, if using, on both sides of the chops. Cook over medium-high heat on a portable barbecue or in a grill pan about 5 minutes on each side until crispy on the outside and succulent and juicy inside. Serve hot with the potato salad and mustard.

Prepare ahead: Make the potato salad at home before you leave and store in an airtight container in a cooler up to 2 days.

Fish Kebabs with Paprika Dressing

Vegetarians should replace the fish and pancetta with 14 ounces tofu, cut into bite-size pieces. Add the tofu to the dressing and let marinate in a cooler 30 minutes. Season well with salt and pepper before cooking. Reserve the dressing and serve with the tofu kebabs and pita breads.

SERVES: 4
PREPARATION TIME: 15 MINUTES
COOKING TIME: ABOUT 5 MINUTES

BY THE BEACH

4 ounces pancetta	8 ounces cherry tomatoes	PAPRIKA DRESSING:
1 pound firm white fish,	4 pita breads	juice of 1 lemon
such as monkfish or	salt and pepper	1 garlic clove
pollock, cut into bite-size		¼ cup olive oil
pieces or 14 ounces tofu,		1 teaspoon smoked paprika
cut into bite-size pieces		1 handful of parsley leaves

1 If using wooden skewers, soak them in cold water at least 30 minutes before grilling. Mix together all of the ingredients for the dressing and set aside.

2 Wrap a slice of pancetta around each piece of fish, then thread onto skewers, alternating with the cherry tomatoes. Season with salt and pepper.

3 Cook the kebabs over high heat on a portable barbecue or in a grill pan about 5 minutes, turning regularly. To check the kebabs are cooked, carefully pull back the pancetta to ensure the fish pulls away easily from the skewers.

4 Warm each pita bread over low heat on a portable barbecue or in a grill pan about 30 seconds on each side. Serve the kebabs with the dressing and warmed pita breads.

Seafood Linguine

SERVES: 4
PREPARATION TIME: 20 MINUTES
COOKING TIME: ABOUT 15 MINUTES

heaped 2 cups raw or cooked seafood, such as shrimp and mussels
14 ounces linguine or spaghetti

3 tablespoons olive oil
6 garlic cloves, finely sliced
3 tomatoes or 10 cherry tomatoes, finely chopped

½ red chili, seeded and finely chopped (optional)
2 handfuls of parsley leaves, finely chopped
salt and pepper

1 Peel and devein the shrimp, then scrub the mussels thoroughly with a stiff brush in a bucket of cold water to remove all traces of grit. Remove any barnacles or other traces of debris attached to the shells and pull off and discard the "beard" of fibrous material around the edge. Rinse again and discard any with broken shells and any that do not close as soon as tapped.

2 Cook the pasta in plenty of salted boiling water until al dente.

3 Meanwhile, heat the oil in a skillet over medium heat and add the garlic. Cook about 1 to 2 minutes until just golden, then add the tomatoes and chili, if using, and season with salt and pepper.

4 Tip the mussels into the skillet and cook about 2 minutes, shaking the pan occasionally. Add the shrimp and the parsley leaves and cook 3 minutes longer until the shrimp are pink and cooked through and all the mussels have opened. Discard any mussels that do not open. If using cooked seafood, add to the pan with the parsley leaves and cook about 2 to 3 minutes until the shrimp and mussels are hot.

5 Drain the pasta and return to the pan, then add the seafood sauce and mix thoroughly. Serve hot, sprinkled with pepper.

Grilled Fish & Smoky Eggplant Salad

SERVES: 4
PREPARATION TIME: 25 MINUTES, PLUS 5 TO 10 MINUTES MARINATING
COOKING TIME: ABOUT 25 MINUTES

4 whole sea bream, sea
  bass or mullet, gutted
  and cleaned
2 chilies, finely sliced
1 handful of parsley leaves,
  finely chopped
crusty bread, to serve

EGGPLANT SALAD:
2 large eggplants
2 red or yellow bell
  peppers
7 ounces cherry tomatoes,
  quartered
1 handful of parsley leaves,
  finely chopped

MARINADE:
juice of 1 lemon or ¼ cup
  Marinade Base (page 21)
2 garlic cloves, crushed
4 teaspoons ground cumin
¼ cup olive oil
salt and pepper

1 Cook the eggplants and peppers over a hot flaming portable barbecue or a naked gas flame about 15 minutes, turning occasionally, until the skin is charred and flaky, and the flesh is very soft. (Chargrilling the eggplants will release an irresistible, smoky flavour.) Set aside and let cool.

2 Meanwhile, mix together all of the ingredients for the marinade in a bowl and season with salt and pepper. Using a sharp knife, make 2 or 3 diagonal cuts on each side of the fish. Put the fish, chilies, parsley leaves and half of the marinade in a plastic freezer bag. Seal the bag, then rub the marinade all over the fish and let marinate in a cooler 5 to 10 minutes.

3 When the eggplants are cool enough to handle, scoop out the flesh, discarding the skin and squeeze out as much liquid as possible. Discard the liquid and coarsely chop the flesh. Remove and discard the cores from the peppers, then slice the flesh. Put the eggplants, peppers, cherry tomatoes, parsley leaves and the remaining marinade in a large bowl and toss well.

4 Transfer the fish to a portable barbecue or grill pan. Cook over medium heat about 4 to 5 minutes on each side until a skewer inserted into the thickest part of the flesh meets no resistance. Serve immediately with the eggplant salad and crusty bread.

Paella

SERVES: 4
PREPARATION TIME: 15 MINUTES
COOKING TIME: ABOUT 40 MINUTES

2 tablespoons olive oil
1 onion, finely chopped
2 red bell peppers, seeded
   and sliced
3 garlic cloves, finely
   chopped
1 teaspoon smoked paprika
7 ounces chorizo, chopped

heaped 2 cups paella rice
4⅓ cups chicken stock
a pinch of saffron
heaped 1 cup defrosted,
   frozen peas
7 ounces raw jumbo
   shrimp, shell and head
   on or cooked jumbo
   shrimp

1 handful of parsley leaves,
   chopped
salt and pepper
lemon wedges, to serve

BY THE BEACH

1 Heat the oil in a large skillet over medium heat. Add the onion and cook
   about 5 minutes until it starts to soften. Add the peppers and garlic, season
   with salt and pepper and cook 5 minutes longer until the vegetables are soft.
2 Stir in the paprika and chorizo, cook 1 minute, then add the rice and mix.
   Make sure everything is well combined before adding the stock and saffron.
   Bring to a boil over high heat, then put the pan over low heat and simmer
   about 20 to 25 minutes, until the rice is just tender and most of the liquid
   has been absorbed. Add a little water if the paella becomes dry.
3 Add the peas and shrimp and cook about 5 minutes until the shrimp are pink
   and cooked through. If using cooked shrimp, cook about 2 to 3 minutes until
   hot. Season to taste with salt and pepper and stir in the parsley leaves. Serve
   hot with lemon wedges.

Moules Marinière

SERVES: 4
PREPARATION TIME: 30 MINUTES
COOKING TIME: ABOUT 30 MINUTES

4 pounds 8 ounces mussels
¼ cup (½ stick) butter
2 onions, chopped
2 garlic cloves, finely
   chopped
1 teaspoon pepper

2 handfuls of parsley
   leaves, finely chopped
generous 1¼ cups dry
   white wine
¼ cup crème fraîche
   (optional)
crusty bread, to serve

1 Scrub the mussels thoroughly with a stiff brush in a bucket of cold water to remove all traces of grit, then remove any barnacles or other traces of debris attached to the shells and pull off and discard the "beard" of fibrous material around the edge. Rinse again and discard any with broken shells and any that do not close as soon as tapped.

2 Heat the butter in a large saucepan over medium heat until melted. Add the onions and garlic and cook about 7 to 8 minutes until softened but not browned. Stir in the pepper and three-quarters of the parsley leaves, then pour in the wine and scant ¾ cup water. Bring to a boil, then put the pan over low heat and simmer about 15 minutes until the liquid has reduced slightly.

3 Put the pan over high heat and return to a boil. Tip the mussels into the pan and cover with a lid. Cook about 5 minutes, shaking the pan occasionally, until all the mussels have opened. Discard any mussels that do not open. Remove the pan from the heat and stir in the crème fraîche, if using, and the remaining parsley leaves. Serve hot with crusty bread to mop up all sauce.

Butternut Squash Tagine with Nut & Raisin Couscous

SERVES: 4
PREPARATION TIME: 10 MINUTES
COOKING TIME: ABOUT 30 MINUTES

1 tablespoon olive oil
1 large onion, finely chopped
1 teaspoon garam masala
1 large butternut squash, peeled and cubed
1 garlic clove, finely chopped
1 teaspoon harissa paste, plus extra to serve

1 teaspoon salt
1 red bell pepper, seeded and cut into large chunks
3¼ cups canned diced tomatoes
1 teaspoon pepper
1 handful of cilantro leaves, chopped

NUT & RAISIN COUSCOUS:
heaped 2 cups couscous
½ cup raisin and nut mix, such as pine nuts, sliced almonds or shelled pistachios
2 tablespoons olive oil
salt and pepper

1 Heat the oil in a saucepan over medium heat. Add the onion and cook about 5 minutes until it starts to soften. Add the garam masala and cook about 1 minute, then add the butternut squash, garlic, harissa paste and salt. Cover with a lid and cook 2 minutes longer.

2 Put the pan over high heat, add the red pepper, canned tomatoes and pepper and bring to a boil. Put the pan over low heat, cover with a lid and simmer about 20 minutes until the squash is tender.

3 Meanwhile, put the couscous, raisins and nuts in a large bowl and pour over scant 2½ cups boiled water. Season with salt and pepper and cover immediately. Let soak at least 5 minutes until the grains are tender. Fluff up the couscous with a fork, then add the oil and mix well.

4 Stir the cilantro leaves into the tagine and serve hot with the couscous and extra harissa paste.

Fruit Kebabs with Mint & Black Pepper Syrup

SERVES: 4
PREPARATION TIME: 10 MINUTES
COOKING TIME: ABOUT 10 MINUTES

1 small pineapple, peeled and cut into bite-size chunks

2 kiwis, peeled and cut into bite-size chunks

2 bananas, peeled and cut into bite-size chunks

2 tablespoons (¼ stick) butter, softened

MINT & BLACK PEPPER SYRUP:
¼ cup sugar, any variety
1 small handful of mint leaves, finely chopped
1 teaspoon pepper

1 If using wooden skewers, soak them in cold water at least 30 minutes before grilling. Thread the fruit onto skewers, then smear the butter all over the kebabs with your fingers.

2 To make the syrup, put the sugar and 2 tablespoons water in a saucepan over low heat. Cook, stirring frequently, about 4 minutes until the sugar dissolves. Let the sugar mixture bubble until it thickens into syrup and colors slightly. Remove the pan from the heat and stir in the mint leaves and pepper.

3 Meanwhile, cook the fruit skewers over high heat on a portable barbecue or in a grill pan about 2 to 3 minutes, turning occasionally, until just starting to brown. Serve hot with the sticky syrup drizzled over the top.

Mango & Passion Fruit Fool

Try to find Pakistani honey mangoes for this recipe—they are small, yellow and sweet. If you do find them, you won't need to add extra honey to taste. If you can't get hold of any passion fruit, raspberries are a great alternative.

SERVES: 4
PREPARATION TIME: 10 MINUTES

2 mangoes, such as honey mangoes, peeled, pitted and finely chopped

4 passion fruit or scant 1⅓ cups raspberries
heaped 2 cups thick plain yogurt

honey, to taste

1 Put the mango in a large bowl. Cut each passion fruit in half and scoop out the flesh and seeds into the bowl with the mango.
2 Divide the yogurt into bowls and top with the mango and passion fruit mixture. Taste and add a little honey, if you like, and serve.

Campsite Mess

Eton Mess for the big outdoors.

SERVES: 4
PREPARATION TIME: 5 MINUTES

4 ready-made meringues or meringue nests	heaped 2 cups chopped fruit, such as strawberries	generous 1 cup crème fraîche or thick heavy cream

1 Break the meringues into a large bowl and gently stir in the fruit and crème fraîche. Serve immediately.

S'mores

A great American invention that we first tried with our cousins.

SERVES: 4
PREPARATION TIME: 5 MINUTES
COOKING TIME: ABOUT 5 MINUTES

8 marshmallows	3½ ounces chocolate, any variety, broken into squares	16 biscuits, such as graham crackers

1 If using wooden skewers, soak them in cold water at least 30 minutes before grilling. Thread 2 marshmallows onto the end of each skewer and toast them over a portable barbecue, open fire or a gas flame about 3 minutes until golden on the outside. Don't toast them too close to the flame or they will burn.
2 To make a s'more, sandwich 1 hot toasted marshmallow and 1 square of chocolate between 2 graham crackers. Repeat with the remaining ingredients and serve while the marshmallows and chocolate are gooey.

Sticky Toffee Bananas

This is a really quick dessert to prepare and is enormously satisfying and warming—particularly if you add the rum!

SERVES: 4
PREPARATION TIME: 5 MINUTES
COOKING TIME: ABOUT 5 MINUTES

¼ cup (½ stick) butter
4 bananas, peeled and cut
  into diagonal slices

2 tablespoons honey, light
  corn syrup or sugar, any
  variety
2 tablespoons orange juice

1 tablespoon rum (optional)
crème fraîche or custard,
  to serve

1 Heat the butter in a skillet over medium heat until melted. Add the bananas and cook about 3 to 4 minutes, turning occasionally, until they start to brown.
2 Add the honey, orange juice and rum, if using, and cook 1 minute longer until the liquid starts to simmer. Serve hot with crème fraîche.

IN THE COUNTRY

In the Country

Where there are farms, there are usually farm stores or farmers' markets, so camping in the countryside opens up a world of possibilities when it comes to cooking and eating. You can find fantastically fresh vegetables, meat and dairy products, and you may even find the opportunity to forage for wild herbs, mushrooms or fruit.

Being in the countryside often involves long walks, lots of fresh air and other outdoor activities, so you'll need heartier dishes to see you through the day. Why not try the delicious Sicilian Sausage Pasta (page 122), especially if you can get hold of some locally produced fresh pork sausage, or the heart-warming slow-cooked Shin of Beef Potjie (page 116) — a sumptuous South African meat and vegetable stew that's best cooked over the embers of a portable charcoal barbecue or open fire.

Eggs and cheese feature heavily in this chapter, from the indulgent Cheese Fondue (page 127) to the lighter Pear & Blue Cheese Salad (page 115). Take the key ingredients listed below and you can turn fresh, local products into delicious camping dishes. Even better, follow our carefully worked out meal plans to make countryside cooking a breeze.

KEY INGREDIENTS

- allspice, ground
- bouillon cubes
- brown sugar and/or honey
- chilies and/or chili sauce
- cinnamon
- fennel seeds
- garam masala
- garlic
- ginger root
- herbs, fresh (cilantro leaves, mint leaves and parsley leaves)
- lemons
- limes
- Marinade Base (page 21)
- nutmeg
- olive oil and/or sunflower oil
- salt and pepper
- soy sauce
- Vinaigrette (page 21)
- wine, dry white

TIPS

Building and lighting an open fire

A campfire is the heart of the camping experience and the very essence of its back-to-basics appeal. A good campfire provides warmth and light, but is also a place to congregate, tell stories, play music and, of course, to cook. When planning and researching your camping vacation look out for the campgrounds that allow open fires—many do, although the drier the climate, the less likely campfires will be allowed because the risk of the fire spreading becomes too great. Many campgrounds have fire pits or fire rings, though others will only let you have a fire in a brazier or your barbecue grill.

To light your fire, it goes without saying that you need copious amounts of dry wood: small pieces to act as kindling and get the fire going, and larger logs to provide the sustained heat and light. Children love gathering up the kindling, but just in case there's not much around, bring some kindling twigs with you. Check whether your camp store provides firewood; if not, then bring this as well. Matches and newspaper for tinder are also vital. The most reliable approach for lighting a fire is the cone or teepee method:

1 Scrunch up balls of newspaper and arrange the kindling twigs in a cone shape around and leaning on the newspaper.
2 Arrange the logs or larger pieces in a larger cone around the kindling so the tops of the logs are supporting each other.
3 Light the newpaper and then as the logs begin to burn, push them into the center of the fire. If all else fails, there's no shame in resorting to firestarters!

Remember

1 Watch out for the gaps between the logs—too big and they will not catch fire, too close and they won't be able to breathe.
2 Safety is paramount. Before you light, make sure that the fire area is cleared of things that could help the fire spread such as branches or leaves. Surrounding the pit with stones is a good idea. Don't leave the fire unsupervised, especially when there are children around, and always put it out before you go to bed.

🍴 Meal Plan for Young Kids

FRIDAY DINNER	• Lamb Kofta with Tahini Sauce (page 121) 🏠 • Rice Pudding with Raspberry Jam (page 132)
SATURDAY BREAKFAST	• French Toast with Apricot Filling (page 104)
SATURDAY LUNCH	• Mexican Salad (page 113) 🏠
SATURDAY DINNER	• Sicilian Sausage Pasta (page 122) • Gorp Balls with Moroccan Mint Tea (page 131) 🏠
SUNDAY BREAKFAST	• Cheesy Breakfast Omelet (page 107)
SUNDAY LUNCH	• Campfire Quesadilla Calzone (page 110)

SHOPPING LIST

Spices & Flavorings
allspice, ground (½ tsp.)
cinnamon (½ tsp.)
fennel seeds (1 tbsp.)
honey, clear (2 tbsp.)
olive oil (1 bottle)
salt & pepper
sugar, granulated (¾ cup)
wine (¾ cup)

Cans & Jars
apricot jam (1 jar)
chickpeas (14½ oz.)
diced tomatoes
  (1 lb. 12 oz.)
kidney beans (14½ oz.)
olives, black pitted
  (1¼ cups)
peanut butter (1 jar)
raspberry jam (1 jar)

tahini (½ cup)
tomato paste (4½ oz.)

Dry Foods
bread (1 large sliced loaf)
dried fruit (1¼ cups)
nuts, chopped (1¼ cups)
pasta, penne (4 cups)
pita breads (4)
short-grain rice (1¼ cups)
soft flour tortillas, large (8)
tortilla chips, lightly salted
  (1 bag)

Meat
chicken breast filets (2)
fresh pork sausage (14 oz.)
ham, cooked (9 oz.)
lamb, ground (1 lb. 2 oz.)

Chilled Foods
butter (2¼ sticks)
cheddar cheese (11½ oz.)
eggs, extra large (11)
milk (1 quart)
mozzarella cheese (1 lb. 2 oz.)
Parmesan cheese (3½ oz.)
sour cream (1 cup)

Fruit & Vegetables
avocados (2)
chilies (3)
cucumber (½)
garlic cloves (5)
lemons (2)
lettuce, large crunchy head (1)
lime (1)
mint leaves (4 handfuls)
onions, large (2)
parsley leaves (4 handfuls)
tomatoes (2)

IN THE COUNTRY

🍴 Meal Plan for Older Kids

FRIDAY DINNER	• Chargrilled Tuna with Thai Dressing (page 125) 🏠 • Sticky Figs in Foil (page 133)
SATURDAY BREAKFAST	• French Toast with Apricot Filling (page 104)
SATURDAY LUNCH	• Chinese Omelet (page 114)
SATURDAY DINNER	• Indian Lamb Chops with Rice & Lentils (page 120) 🏠 • Chargrilled Fruit on Cinnamon Toast (page 128) 🏠
SUNDAY BREAKFAST	• One-Pan Full English Breakfast (page 106)
SUNDAY LUNCH	• Campfire Quesadilla Calzone (page 110)

SHOPPING LIST

Spices & Flavorings
cinnamon (2 tsp.)
garam masala (2 tsp.)
olive oil (1 bottle)
salt & pepper
soy sauce (2 tbsp.)
sugar, brown (¾ cup)
Thai fish sauce (2 tbsp.)

Cans & Jars
apricot jam (1 jar)
chutney, mango (1 jar)
lentils, brown (14½ oz.)
olives, black pitted
  (1¼ cups)
tomato paste (4½ oz.)

Dry Foods
basmati rice (1¼ cups)
soft flour tortillas, large (8)
sourdough bread, sliced
  (1 large loaf)

Meat & Fish
bacon (8 slices)
ham, cooked (9 oz.)
lamb chops (12)
sausages (4)
shrimp, cooked peeled (8 oz.)
tuna steaks (4)

Chilled Foods
butter (3¼ sticks)
eggs, extra large (15)
milk (¼ cup)

mozzarella cheese
  (1 lb. 2 oz.)
noodles, fine fresh (10½ oz.)
yogurt, thick plain (1½ cups)

Fruit & Vegetables
bean sprouts (4 cups)
carrots (2)
chilies (2)
chives (12)
cilantro leaves (2 handfuls)
cucumber, small (1)
figs (4)
garlic cloves (4)
ginger root (1-in. piece)
limes (2)
plums, large (4)
tomatoes, large (2)

IN THE COUNTRY

🍴 Meal Plan for Vegetarians

FRIDAY DINNER	• Cheese Fondue (page 127) • Sticky Figs in Foil (page 133)
SATURDAY BREAKFAST	• Herby Wild Mushrooms (page 109)
SATURDAY LUNCH	• Pear & Blue Cheese Salad (page 115) 🏠
SATURDAY DINNER	• Risotto Primavera (page 126) • Gorp Balls with Moroccan Mint Tea (page 131) 🏠
SUNDAY BREAKFAST	• Cheesy Breakfast Omelet (page 107)
SUNDAY LUNCH	• Mexican Salad (page 113) 🏠

SHOPPING LIST

Spices & Flavorings
chili sauce (1 bottle)
cinnamon (½ tsp.)
honey (2 tbsp.)
olive oil (1 bottle)
salt & pepper
sugar, any variety
  (½ cup)
vegetable bouillon cubes (2)
Vinaigrette (¼ cup),
  (page 21)
wine, dry white
  (1½ cups)

Cans & Jars
kidney beans (14½ oz.)
peanut butter (1 jar)
pickles (1 jar)

Dry Foods
baguettes (4)
bread, crusty (1 loaf)
cornstarch (1 tbsp.)
dried fruit (1¼ cups)
nuts, chopped (1¼ cup)
risotto rice (1¼ cups)
tortilla chips, lightly salted
  (1 bag)
walnut pieces (1¼ cups)

Chilled Foods
blue cheese (8 oz.)
butter (2¼ sticks)
cheddar cheese (4½ oz.)
eggs, extra large (8)
Emmental cheese (15 oz.)
Gruyère cheese (8 oz.)
Parmesan cheese (5½ oz.)

sour cream (½ cup)
yogurt, thick plain (1¼ cups)

Fruit & Vegetables
avocados (2)
early Summer vegetable mix,
  such as asparagus, zucchini
  & peas (1 lb. 5 oz.)
figs (4)
garlic cloves (5)
lemon (1)
lettuce, large crunchy head (1)
lime (1)
mint leaves (4 handfuls)
mushrooms (1 lb.)
onion, red (1)
parsley leaves (3 handfuls)
pears (8)
salad greens (7–8 cups)

IN THE COUNTRY

French Toast with Apricot Filling

Here is a great opportunity to sample locally produced jam. We've suggested apricot, but any will do—our son loves it with greengage jam. Alternatively, this makes a brilliant savory snack. Just omit the sugar from the recipe and fill the sandwich with relish.

SERVES: 4
PREPARATION TIME: 5 MINUTES
COOKING TIME: ABOUT 10 MINUTES

8 slices of bread
3 extra large eggs, beaten
¼ cup milk

1 teaspoon sugar, any
    variety, plus extra for
    sprinkling

¼ cup apricot jam
¼ cup (½ stick) butter,
    plus extra for buttering
    the bread

1 Butter one side of each slice of bread. In a bowl, beat together the eggs, milk and sugar. Use the buttered slices of bread and jam to make 4 sandwiches, each filled with 1 tablespoon of jam.

2 Melt half of the butter in a large skillet over medium heat. Dip the sandwiches into the egg mixture, turning to coat on both sides, until the bread absorbs some of the mixture.

3 Working in batches, cook the French toast about 2 minutes on each side until golden. Remove from the pan and repeat with the remaining butter and French toast. Serve hot, sprinkled with extra sugar.

One-Pan Full English Breakfast

SERVES: 4
PREPARATION TIME: 5 MINUTES
COOKING TIME: ABOUT 25 MINUTES

2 tablespoons (¼ stick)
   butter or sunflower oil,
   plus extra for making
   fried bread if needed

4 sausages
2 large tomatoes, halved
8 bacon slices

4 slices of bread, any
   variety, sliced in half
4 extra large eggs
salt and pepper

1 Heat half of the butter in a large skillet over medium heat. Add the sausages to the pan and cook, turning occasionally, about 5 minutes. Season the tomatoes with salt and pepper. Add to the pan, cut-side down, and cook 5 minutes longer.

2 Using grill tongs, turn the tomatoes and sausages over, then push them to the side of the skillet and add the bacon. Fry about 2 to 3 minutes on each side until golden. Push the bacon to the side of the pan, piling the cooked meat on top of the meat that needs a little longer to cook.

3 To make fried bread, add 1 tablespoon of butter to the skillet. Cook the slices of bread about 5 minutes until golden on the bottom. The other side of your fried bread will cook at the same time as the eggs, so turn each slice and push to the side of the pan, piling the rest of the cooked food on top. Alternatively, toast the bread over low heat on a portable babecue grill or metal grill rack over an open fire, or in a grill pan, about 1 to 2 minutes on each side until crisp and golden brown.

4 Add the remaining butter to the skillet and crack in the eggs, spacing them apart. Season the eggs with salt and pepper. Cook, occasionally spooning hot oil over the top of each egg, about 3 minutes until the whites are set. Divide all the ingredients onto plates and serve hot.

Cheesy Breakfast Omelet

This is the classic omelet folded over with a cheese filling, like they serve in France. Don't wait for everyone to be served before you eat it as it's best hot from the pan. It's especially delicious served with crusty bread.

SERVES: 4
PREPARATION TIME: 5 MINUTES
COOKING TIME: ABOUT 8 MINUTES

8 extra large eggs
2 tablespoons (¼ stick)
  butter

7 ounces hard cheese, such
  as Emmental or cheddar,
  grated or finely sliced

salt and pepper
bread, any variety, to serve

1 Beat the eggs together in a bowl and season with salt and pepper. Melt half of the butter in a large skillet over medium heat, tilting the pan to evenly coat the bottom.

2 When the butter starts to froth, add half of the egg mixture to the pan, shaking the pan to evenly coat the bottom. Cook about 2 minutes until the omelet is firm and golden brown on the bottom and a little runny on top.

3 Sprinkle half of the cheese over the top of the omelet. Using a spatula, fold the omelet in half to enclose the cheese. Cook 1 minute longer. Transfer to a plate and serve, or cover with tinfoil to keep warm. Repeat with the remaining butter, egg mixture and cheese to make another omelet.

4 Cut the omelets in half and serve hot with bread.

Herby Wild Mushrooms

There's something hugely romantic about foraging for your own mushrooms. If you're not a confident forager, it's vital that you have a very good guide book with pictures. Remember, if you're not sure, don't eat it. If you don't have any butter, fry the mushrooms in olive or sunflower oil instead.

SERVES: 4
PREPARATION TIME: 10 MINUTES
COOKING TIME: ABOUT 10 MINUTES

2 tablespoons olive oil
¼ cup (½ stick) butter
1 pound mushrooms, wiped
   clean and quartered
3 garlic cloves, finely
   sliced

slices of crusty bread or
   baguette
3 handfuls of parsley
   leaves, finely chopped
juice of ¼ lemon
salt and pepper

1 Heat the oil and butter in a large skillet over medium heat. Add the mushrooms and cook, without stirring, about 2 to 3 minutes until starting to brown.

2 Stir in the garlic and season with salt and pepper. Cook about 3 to 5 minutes until golden brown.

3 Meanwhile, warm or lightly toast the bread over low heat on a portable barbecue or in a grill pan about 1 to 2 minutes on each side until crisp and golden brown.

4 Stir in the parsley leaves and remove the pan from the heat, then add the lemon juice and stir 30 seconds longer. Serve immediately, letting the warmed slices of crusty bread soak up all the juices.

Campfire Quesadilla Calzone

This isn't a pizza, but it's a very good camping alternative. Our kids love this filling, but you can experiment with other fillings, such as salami, arugula and grated cheese.

MAKES: 8
PREPARATION TIME: 10 MINUTES
COOKING TIME: ABOUT 30 MINUTES

½ cup tomato paste
¼ cup olive oil
2 garlic cloves, crushed
8 large soft flour tortillas

9 ounces cooked ham, finely sliced
1 pound 2 ounces mozzarella cheese, drained and sliced

heaped 1 cup pitted black olives, halved
1 chili, seeded and finely chopped
salt and pepper

1 Heat a large skillet over medium heat. Put the tomato paste, oil and garlic in a bowl. Mix well, adding water 1 tablespoon at a time, until the mixture is smooth enough to spread. Season with salt and pepper.

2 Put 1 tortilla in the pan and spread 1 tablespoon of the tomato mixture over the top. Sprinkle one-eighth of the ham, mozzarella, olives and chili over half of the tortilla. Try to sprinkle the cheese around the edge of the tortilla—it will help the quesadilla hold together when you flip it. Using a spatula, fold the tortilla in half to enclose the filling, pressing down the edges to seal.

3 Cook about 1 to 2 minutes, then flip the quesadilla over and cook 2 minutes longer until the cheese has melted and the tortilla is beginning to crisp. Repeat with the remaining ingredients to make 8 quesadillas. Serve hot.

Mexican Salad

This is a great salad—and it's just as good without the chicken.

SERVES: 4
PREPARATION TIME: 20 MINUTES
COOKING TIME: ABOUT 10 MINUTES

2 boneless, skinless
   chicken breast filets
olive oil, for brushing
1 large crunchy head of
   lettuce, coarsely torn
2 avocados, peeled, pitted
   and chopped

14½ ounces canned kidney
   beans, drained
heaped 1 cup grated
   cheddar cheese
1 bag of lightly salted
   tortilla chips, roughly
   crushed
salt and pepper

MEXICAN SALAD DRESSING:
½ garlic clove, crushed
juice of ½ lime
½ cup sour cream
1 tablespoon olive oil
a splash of chili sauce or
   ½ chili, seeded and
   finely chopped
salt and pepper

1 Put the chicken breasts in a large plastic freezer bag. Using a camping mallet, slightly flatten the chicken, then brush with oil and season with salt and pepper. Cook over high heat on a portable barbecue or in a grill pan about 5 minutes on each side until beautifully charred and the juices from the chicken run clear when the thickest part of the meat is pierced with the tip of a sharp knife or skewer. Remove from the heat, slice and let cool a little.

2 To make the dressing, put all of the ingredients in a bowl and beat with a fork to form a smooth paste. Season lightly with salt and pepper, bearing in mind that the tortilla chips will be salty, and mix well.

3 Put the sliced chicken and all of the remaining ingredients in a large bowl. Drizzle over the salad dressing and toss to combine. Serve immediately.

Prepare ahead: Make the dressing at home before you leave and store in a cooler up to 2 days.

Chinese Omelet

This is an old favorite of ours that we often have as a midweek dinner, but it also works very well as a hearty camping lunch. If your skillet is small, cook the omelet in two batches, and reduce the cooking time by 1 minute on both sides. Leave out the noodles for a lighter meal.

SERVES: 4
PREPARATION TIME: 5 MINUTES
COOKING TIME: ABOUT 12 MINUTES

8 extra large eggs, beaten
8 ounces cooked peeled
  shrimp
3 tablespoons chopped
  chives or 3 scallions,
  chopped

2 tablespoons soy sauce
½ chili, seeded and finely
  chopped or a splash of
  chili sauce

2 tablespoons (¼ stick)
  butter or sunflower oil
10½ ounces fine fresh
  noodles

1 Beat the eggs together in a large bowl. Add the shrimp, chives, soy sauce and chili and mix well.
2 Heat the butter in a large skillet over medium heat. Add the noodles and cook 2 minutes, shaking the pan to form an even layer. Pour in the egg mixture, spreading the shrimp out evenly. Cook about 5 minutes until the omelet is firm and golden brown on the bottom.
3 Remove the skillet from the heat and turn the omelet out onto a plate. Slide the omelet back into the pan, runny-side down, and cook 5 minutes longer or until golden brown and set. Cut into wedges and serve hot, straight from the pan.

Pear & Blue Cheese Salad

We devised this recipe when we went camping in Normandy, France—and gathered all the ingredients from the local farmers' market.

SERVES: 4
PREPARATION TIME: 15 MINUTES

7–8 cups salad greens, such as watercress, baby spinach and arugula
¼ cup Vinaigrette (page 21)
heaped 1 cup walnut pieces, chopped

8 pears, peeled, cored and sliced
8 ounces blue cheese, such as Roquefort, Stilton or Gorgonzola, crumbled

slices of baguette or crusty bread, to serve

1 Put the salad greens, vinaigrette and walnuts in a large bowl and toss gently but thoroughly. Divide the salad onto plates.
2 Top each salad with slices of pear, then sprinkle the crumbled cheese over the top. Serve with slices of baguette.

 Prepare ahead: Make the Vinaigrette (page 21) at home before you leave.

Shin of Beef Potjie

This is Afrikaner outdoor cooking at its best. Potjie (pronounced poike) is a stew made in a big cast-iron pot and cooked very slowly over embers. Don't worry if you don't have a camping pot or a heavy-bottomed saucepan with you—any pot with a lid will do.

SERVES: 4
PREPARATION TIME: 15 MINUTES
COOKING TIME: AT LEAST 3 HOURS

2 pounds 4 ounces shin of beef, bone removed and trimmed of fat, or chuck steak, cut into chunks
2 onions, peeled
2 large carrots, cut into chunks
12 ounces rutabaga, parsnip, celeriac, turnip or leek chunks
4 tomatoes, chopped
4 garlic cloves, peeled
1 bay leaf (optional)
1 rosemary sprig (optional)
1 thyme sprig (optional)
½ bottle of red wine
4 large baking potatoes
salt and pepper
butter, to serve

1 Put the beef in a large heavy-bottomed saucepan or camping pot and place the onions in the center of the meat. Season well with pepper and add a few pinches of salt, then top with the vegetables, garlic and herbs, if using.
2 Pour in the wine, then add enough water to almost cover the ingredients. Cover with a lid and cook over very low heat at least 3 hours, preferably 5 hours.
3 Meanwhile, wrap each potato in tinfoil. Cook about 45 minutes in the glowing embers of a portable charcoal barbecue or open fire until cooked through and the skins are crisp, then split open. Remember to move the potatoes from time to time to let them cook evenly. Alternatively, chop the potatoes and cook in plenty of salted boiling water about 10 minutes until soft. Remove from the heat and drain well, then return to the pan and roughly mash with a fork. Just before serving, top the baked potatoes or the fork-mashed potatoes with a little butter and season with salt and pepper. Serve immediately with the warm, meltingly tender stew.

Barbecued Steak with Camping Butter

The anchovies in this recipe don't taste remotely fishy, they just give the butter a delicious, savory flavor. If you don't want to cook the potatoes, serve the steaks in crusty bread spread with Camping Butter.

SERVES: 4
PREPARATION TIME: 10 MINUTES
COOKING TIME: ABOUT 45 MINUTES

4 large baking potatoes
4 tenderloin steaks
salt and pepper
salad, to serve

CAMPING BUTTER:
¼ cup (½ stick) butter, softened
1½ jarred or canned anchovy fillets, drained

2 teaspoons Marinade Base (page 21)
1 handful of parsley leaves, finely chopped

1 Wrap each potato in tinfoil. Cook about 45 minutes in the glowing embers of a portable charcoal barbecue or open fire until cooked through and the skins are crisp, then split open. Remember to move the potatoes from time to time to let them cook evenly. Alternatively, chop the potatoes and cook in plenty of salted boiling water about 10 minutes until soft. Remove from the heat and drain well, then return to the pan and roughly mash with a fork.

2 Meanwhile, make the camping butter. Mash together the butter, anchovies, Marinade Base and parsley leaves in a bowl. Cover and set aside.

3 Season the steaks well on both sides with salt and pepper. Cook over high heat on a portable barbecue or in a grill pan about 2 to 4 minutes on each side until cooked to your liking. The steaks should be charred and crispy on the outside and succulent on the inside.

4 Just before serving, top the steaks and the baked potatoes or the fork-mashed potatoes with a little camping butter. Serve hot with salad.

IN THE COUNTRY

Indian Lamb Chops with Rice & Lentils

SERVES: 4
PREPARATION TIME: 15 MINUTES, PLUS AT LEAST 1 HOUR MARINATING
COOKING TIME: ABOUT 20 MINUTES

12 lamb chops
heaped 1 cup basmati rice
14½ ounces canned brown
   or green lentils, drained
salt and pepper
mango chutney or eggplant
   pickle, to serve

MARINADE:
2 teaspoons garam masala
1 teaspoon brown sugar
1 teaspoon salt
2 garlic cloves, crushed
juice of 1 lime or ¼ cup
   Marinade Base, made
   with lime juice (page 21)

½ chili, seeded and finely
   chopped or ½ teaspoon
   dried chili flakes
2 tablespoons thick plain
   yogurt, plus extra to
   serve
1 handful of cilantro leaves,
   chopped

1 To make the marinade, put the garam masala, brown sugar, salt, garlic, lime juice, chili, yogurt and cilantro leaves in a large plastic freezer bag. Add the lamb chops and seal the bag. Rub the marinade all over the lamb and let marinate in a cooler at least 1 hour, preferably overnight.

2 Put the rice and generous 1½ cups water in a saucepan and season with salt and pepper. Bring to a boil over high heat, then cover with a tight-fitting lid and put the pan over low heat. Cook about 10 minutes until all the liquid has been absorbed. Stir in the lentils, then cover and set aside.

3 Cook the marinated lamb chops over high heat on a portable barbecue or in a grill pan about 5 minutes on each side until charred on the outside but pink in the middle. Serve hot with the rice and lentils, yogurt and chutney.

 Prepare ahead: Make the marinade at home before you leave and store in a cooler up to 2 days. You could even take the lamb chops in the marinade if you're planning to eat them on the first night.

Lamb Kofta with Tahini Sauce

SERVES: 4
PREPARATION TIME: 20 MINUTES
COOKING TIME: ABOUT 10 MINUTES

1 pound 2 ounces ground
  lamb
1 large white or red onion,
  finely chopped
½ teaspoon ground
  allspice
½ teaspoon cinnamon

2 handfuls of parsley
  leaves, finely chopped
salt and pepper
4 pita breads, to serve
1 recipe quantity Chickpea
  Salad (page 41), to serve

TAHINI SAUCE:
½ cup tahini
juice of 1 lemon
1 garlic clove, crushed
salt and pepper

1 If using wooden skewers, soak them in cold water at least 30 minutes before grilling. Put the ground lamb, onion, spices and parsley leaves in a bowl, season well with salt and pepper and mix thoroughly. Using your hands, divide the mixture into 8 equal pieces and shape each one into a ball. Mold each ball into a long sausage shape around a skewer to make 8 kofta skewers and set aside.

2 To make the sauce, put the tahini in a bowl and gradually stir in the lemon juice and garlic to make a smooth paste. Season with salt and pepper, then slowly add ½ cup water to make a runny sauce. Set aside.

3 Cook the kofta skewers over high heat on a portable barbecue or in a grill pan about 8 to 10 minutes, turning frequently, until cooked to your liking. Serve hot with the tahini sauce, pita breads and a Chickpea Salad.

 Prepare ahead: Make the Tahini Sauce at home before you leave and store in a cooler up to 1 week. You could use ¼ cup Marinade Base (page 21) instead of the lemon juice and garlic.

IN THE COUNTRY

Sicilian Sausage Pasta

This is one of the most satisfyingly delicious pasta dishes ever, and a total favorite with our kids and all their friends. The fennel seeds make it completely irresistible, so it's worth preparing them properly. Put them in a plastic freezer bag, then seal and crush them with a camping mallet or stone.

SERVES: 4
PREPARATION TIME: 10 MINUTES
COOKING TIME: AT LEAST 35 MINUTES

1 tablespoon olive oil
1 large white or red
  onion, finely chopped
1 garlic clove, finely
  chopped
1 tablespoon fennel seeds,
  crushed

14 ounces fresh pork
  sausage or 6 pork
  sausages, skinned
1 chili, seeded and finely
  chopped
¾ cup red wine or white
  wine
3¼ cups canned diced
  tomatoes

4 cups pasta, such as
  penne or fusilli
2 tablespoons sour cream
salt and pepper
Parmesan cheese shavings,
  to serve

1 Heat the oil in a skillet over medium heat. Add the onion and cook about 5 minutes until softened. Add the garlic, fennel seeds, fresh pork sausage and chili. Using a wooden spoon, break up the fresh pork sausage into small nuggets and cook about 6 to 8 minutes until slightly browned.

2 Add the wine and canned tomatoes to the skillet and then season with salt and pepper. Put the pan over low heat and simmer at least 20 minutes, preferably 40 minutes, to make the meat tender and to thicken the sauce.

3 Meanwhile, cook the pasta in plenty of salted boiling water until al dente. Drain and return to the pan. Just before serving, stir the sour cream into the sauce. Check the seasoning and add extra salt and pepper if needed. Add the pasta to the sauce and mix thoroughly. Serve hot with shavings of Parmesan.

Chargrilled Tuna with Thai Dressing

SERVES: 4
PREPARATION TIME: 10 MINUTES
COOKING TIME: AT LEAST 2 MINUTES

1 recipe quantity Asian
  Salad (page 47)
4 tuna steaks
salt and pepper

THAI DRESSING:
2 tablespoons Thai fish
  sauce
juice of 1 lime
3 teaspoons brown sugar

1-inch piece of ginger root,
  peeled and grated
1 handful of cilantro leaves,
  chopped

1 To make the dressing, put all of the ingredients in a small jar. Secure with a lid and shake vigorously until the brown sugar has completely dissolved. Sprinkle one-third of the dressing over the salad and toss gently but thoroughly, then cover and set aside. Reserve the remaining dressing.

2 Pat the tuna steaks dry with paper towels and season both sides with salt and pepper. Sear over high heat on a portable barbecue or in a grill pan about 1 minute on each side until charred on the outside but pink in the middle, or until cooked to your liking.

3 Remove from the heat and thickly slice each tuna steak. Serve immediately with the salad, and with the reserved dressing drizzled over the top.

Prepare ahead: Make the dressing at home before you leave and store in a cooler up to 3 days.

Risotto Primavera

You can make this risotto with just about any vegetable, including spinach, carrots, celery and leeks. Try to avoid using vegetables that take a long time to cook though, such as butternut squash or beet.

SERVES: 4
PREPARATION TIME: 10 MINUTES
COOKING TIME: ABOUT 30 MINUTES

2 tablespoons olive oil
1 red onion, finely chopped
scant 1¼ cups risotto rice
generous 2½ cups
   vegetable stock

3¼ cups of early summer
   vegetables, such as
   asparagus, zucchini,
   peas and green beans,
   chopped

¼ cup dry white wine
heaped 1 cup grated
   Parmesan cheese, plus
   extra to serve
2 tablespoons (¼ stick)
   butter (optional)
salt and pepper

1 Heat the oil in a large saucepan over medium heat. Add the onion and cook about 5 minutes until softened but not browned. Put the pan over low heat and stir in the risotto rice.

2 Cook, stirring, about 2 minutes, then pour in just enough stock to cover the rice. Cook about 10 minutes, stirring continuously and adding more stock to the pan as the rice absorbs the liquid.

3 Add the vegetables and wine and season with salt and pepper. Cook, stirring occasionally and adding more stock to cover the rice and vegetables, 5 minutes longer until the rice is just tender but retains a slight bite. Stir in the Parmesan and butter, if using, and serve hot with extra Parmesan sprinkled over the top.

Cheese Fondue

Making fondue can be a little tricky as you need to maintain the right temperature to ensure that the sauce stays smooth—too hot and it will solidify into balls, too cold and it goes stringy. But it's the ultimate sharing dish and well worth the effort. Just follow the simple steps below.

SERVES: 4
PREPARATION TIME: 15 MINUTES
COOKING TIME: ABOUT 15 MINUTES

heaped 2 cups grated
  Emmental cheese
heaped 2 cups grated
  Gruyère cheese
1 tablespoon cornstarch or
  all-purpose flour
1 garlic clove, peeled and
  halved

generous 1 cup dry white
  wine, such as Sauvignon
  Blanc
1 tablespoon lemon juice or
  Marinade Base (page 21)
a pinch of nutmeg
  (optional)
pepper

slightly stale crusty
  baguettes, cut into
  cubes, to serve
pickles, to serve
cold cooked meats,
  to serve (optional)

1 Put the cheese and cornstarch in a plastic freezer bag. Seal and shake to coat the cheese with cornstarch, then set aside.

2 Rub the garlic around the inside of a heavy-bottomed saucepan. Add the wine and lemon juice to the pan and bring to a gentle simmer over medium heat.

3 Slowly stir the cheese into the wine, a little at a time, stirring constantly in a zigzag pattern. Cook until the cheese has just melted, taking care not to let the mixture boil as this can cause rubbery balls of cheese to form. (Don't worry if the cheese does start to solidify, you can rescue the fondue with another squeeze of lemon juice or a splash of wine.) Once the mixture is smooth, stir in the nutmeg, if using, and season with pepper, to taste.

4 To serve, keep the pan over very low heat, but take care not to let the fondue cool down too much or it will become stringy and tough. Encourage everyone to spear cubes of bread onto forks or skewers. Dip the bread into the smooth, creamy fondue and enjoy with pickles and cold cooked meats, if you like.

Chargrilled Fruit on Cinnamon Toast

In France they would use vanilla sugar, but this is equally good. Simple, but surprisingly tasty.

SERVES: 4
PREPARATION TIME: 5 MINUTES
COOKING TIME: ABOUT 10 MINUTES

¼ cup sugar, any variety
1 teaspoon cinnamon
4 large plums, apricots, greengages, peaches or nectarines, halved and pitted

4 slices of firm white bread, such as sourdough or ciabatta, lightly buttered on both sides
thick plain yogurt, crème fraîche or custard, to serve

1 Mix together the sugar and cinnamon in a cup and set aside.
2 Grill the plums, cut-side down, over medium heat on a portable barbecue or in a grill pan about 5 minutes until the plums are beginning to turn golden on the bottom.
3 Meanwhile, add the bread to the portable barbecue or grill pan and toast about 2 minutes until golden on the bottom.
4 Turn the plums and slices of bread over and sprinkle the cinnamon sugar over the grilled side of the bread slices and the flesh side of the fruit. Toast the bread 2 minutes longer until golden and transfer to a plate. Cook the plums about 3 minutes until lightly charred and tender. Serve hot on the cinnamon toast with yogurt.

 Prepare ahead: Combine the dry ingredients at home before you leave. Store the mixture in an airtight container up to 1 week.

Gorp Balls with Moroccan Mint Tea

Gorp balls (Good Old Raisins & Peanuts) are great for kids to prepare and are ideal to make outside as they're very messy! You may like to try adding some Granola (page 142) into the mix, in which case add a little extra peanut butter or honey, too.

SERVES: 4
PREPARATION TIME: 15 MINUTES
COOKING TIME: ABOUT 5 MINUTES

heaped 1 cup dried fruit,
  chopped
heaped 1 cup chopped nuts
¼ cup peanut butter
2 tablespoons honey

MOROCCAN MINT TEA:
4 handfuls of mint leaves
4 teaspoons sugar, any
  variety, plus extra to
  taste

1 Put 4⅓ cups water in a saucepan and bring to a boil over high heat. Meanwhile, mix together the dried fruit, nuts, peanut butter and honey in a large bowl. Using your hands, shape the mixture into 12 golf-ball-sized gorp balls or 24 mini gorp balls and set aside.

2 Put the mint leaves in a pitcher and sprinkle in the sugar, then crush with a wooden spoon. Pour the boiled water over the mint leaves and sugar and let stand 5 minutes to let the mint infuse. Add more sugar, if you like, and serve hot with the gorp balls.

Prepare ahead: Make a chopped dried fruit mixture at home before you leave and store in an airtight container up to 1 week. Use it to make the gorp balls, sprinkle it over your Granola with Yogurt & Fruit (page 142) or dip the pieces into a pot of Chocolate Fondue (page 169).

Rice Pudding with Raspberry Jam

On a cool evening, this works really well as a camping dessert, particularly if you've managed to buy some locally produced jam. We think it's every bit as good as the oven-baked version we make at home.

SERVES: 4
PREPARATION TIME: 2 MINUTES
COOKING TIME: ABOUT 30 MINUTES

3¼ cups milk
heaped 1 cup short-grain
   rice
a pinch of salt

3 tablespoons granulated
   sugar
4 to 8 teaspoons raspberry
   jam

1 Put the milk, rice and salt in a heavy-bottomed saucepan and bring to a boil over high heat. Put the pan over low heat and simmer, stirring frequently, about 15 minutes until the rice starts to absorb the milk.

2 Add the sugar and cook, stirring continuously, about 10 minutes until the rice is tender and the pudding has thickened. Pour into bowls and serve hot with the jam spooned over the top.

Sticky Figs in Foil

In this recipe, the butter and sugar caramelize in the tinfoil to create a deliciously sticky dessert. You could try sprinkling some nuts, like pistachios, on top.

SERVES: 4
PREPARATION TIME: 5 MINUTES
COOKING TIME: ABOUT 7 MINUTES

4 figs
½ cup (¼ stick) butter
¼ cup sugar, any variety

½ teaspoon cinnamon
thick plain yogurt or crème
  fraîche, to serve

1 Prepare four squares of tinfoil, each about 6 x 6 inches square. Using a sharp knife, cut a cross in the top of each fig and ease the quarters apart without separating them completely. Put each fig on a square of tinfoil.

2 Put 1 tablespoon of the butter on top of each fig, then sprinkle 1 tablespoon of sugar and a pinch of cinnamon over the top of each one. Pull up the tinfoil to enclose, tightly sealing the seams of the packages. Cook about 5 to 7 minutes in the glowing embers of a portable charcoal barbecue or open fire until the figs are soft. Alternatively, cook the packages over high heat in a grill pan. Remember to move the packages from time to time to let the figs cook evenly. Serve hot with yogurt.

FESTIVALS
& PARTIES

Festivals & Parties

This chapter is all about sharing, having fun, spending time with friends and family, and not being stuck in the kitchen! There are lots of crowd-pleasing, easy-to-prepare dishes like Campfire Chili Con Carne with Yogurt Guacamole & Tortilla Chips (page 157) and Lamb, Eggplant & Mint Tagine (page 158), both of which can easily be made in large batches.

Camping at a festival or in a group is noisy, occasionally chaotic, but great fun. This requires a different approach to cooking. For instance, you may want to prepare your ingredients or even whole dishes in advance—the Campfire Caponata with Garlic Bread (page 153) and Banana Halwa (page 170) are good examples. You may also have less time and opportunity to buy products locally, particularly if you're at a festival or big event. If so, use our meal plans and ready-to-use shopping lists to help you along the way.

To make life as easy as possible we also have lots of food that requires no plates or cutlery, such as Chicken Tikka with Cucumber Raita (page 160) and the Classic Camping Burgers (page 154). These recipes are all about enjoyment. So you could dive into the Chocolate Fondue (page 169), or even relax with some Barbecued Peaches with Hot Chai (page 172).

KEY INGREDIENTS

- bouillon cubes
- brown sugar and/or honey
- chilies, chili sauce or dried chili flakes
- cinnamon and/or allspice, ground
- cumin, ground
- garam masala
- garlic
- ginger root
- herbs, fresh (cilantro leaves, mint leaves and parsley leaves)
- lemons
- limes
- Marinade Base (page 21)
- olive oil and/or sunflower oil
- oregano, dried
- relishes
- salt and pepper
- smoked paprika
- soy sauce
- tomato ketchup
- turmeric
- vinegar (red wine and/or white wine)

TIPS

Cooking for a crowd

Like the rest of the recipes in this book, the quantities given in this section are for four people, but they are the sort of recipes that can be easily doubled or even trebled to cater for larger numbers. It's worth remembering, however, that if you are cooking for more than four, the cooking times will undoubtedly increase—whether you are cooking in batches or simply in greater quantities. It's helpful to be quite organized when cooking for a crowd, with as much as possible prepared before you go—even if it's simply making sure that all the fruit and vegetables are washed. Once you're there have everything laid out and ready to go. And remember, especially if kids have been involved in preparing burgers or skewers, have a bucket of water for washing grubby hands in before getting stuck into the food!

Make a cocktail

Making up a big cocktail is a great way to start a party. We always love making Apricot or Peach Fizz. Here's our recipe with a non-alcoholic version.

16 ice cubes	4⅓ cups lemon soda	1 handful of mint leaves
4⅓ cups apricot juice or peach juice	generous 2 cups sparkling water	vodka or white rum, to taste—for the adults
	juice of 2 limes	

1 If you can get hold of some ice cubes or a block of ice, put the ice into a clean plastic freezer bag (or any clean plastic bag) and bash with your camping mallet.
2 Find the largest pitcher you can, add the ice and pour over the apricot juice, lemon soda and sparkling water.
3 Add the lime juice and mint leaves and serve. For the adult version, simply add vodka or white rum to your taste before serving.

🍴 Meal Plan for Young Kids

FRIDAY DINNER	• Sticky Ribs with Corn on the Cob (page 159) 🏠 • Camping Crepes (with bananas & honey), (page 171) 🏠
SATURDAY BREAKFAST	• Sausage & Potato Hash (page 145)
SATURDAY LUNCH	• Spaghetti Salad (page 152) 🏠
SATURDAY DINNER	• Classic Camping Burgers (page 154) 🏠 • Chocolate Fondue (page 169)
SUNDAY BREAKFAST	• Granola with Yogurt & Fruit (page 142) 🏠
SUNDAY LUNCH	• Mexican Chicken Wraps (page 151) 🏠

SHOPPING LIST

Spices & Flavorings
chili sauce (1 bottle)
honey (1 bottle)
mayonnaise (1 jar)
mustard (1 jar)
olive oil (1 bottle)
salt & pepper
soy sauce (1 tbsp.)
sunflower oil (¼ cup)
tomato ketchup (1 bottle)
white wine vinegar
  (2 tbsp.)

Cans & Jars
anchovy fillets (2)
capers (2 tbsp.)
olives, green pitted
  (½ cup)
pickles (4)

Dry Foods
burger buns (4)
Camping Crepes (4 to 8),
  (page 171)
chocolate (7 oz.)
coconut, shredded (¾ cup)
dried fruit (¾ cup)
marshmallows (1 bag)
nuts and seeds (¾ cup)
rolled oats (1⅔ cups)
soft flour tortillas, large (4)
spaghetti (14 oz.)

Meat
beef, ground (1 lb. 10 oz.)
chicken breast filets (2)
pork ribs (2 racks)
sausages, large (6)

Chilled Foods
butter (2¼ sticks)

cheddar cheese (9 oz.)
eggs, extra large (2)
yogurt, thick plain (2½ cups)

Fruit & Vegetables
arugula leaves (1 handful)
avocado, large (1)
bananas (4)
bell pepper, red (1)
corn on the cob (4)
fruit mix, peaches and
  strawberries (1 lb. 10 oz.)
garlic cloves (5)
lettuce, small crunchy head (1)
lime (1)
onions (3)
parsley leaves (3 handfuls)
potatoes, large (4)
tomatoes (5)

Meal Plan for Older Kids

FRIDAY DINNER	• Chicken Tikka with Cucumber Raita (page 160) 🏠 • Barbecued Peaches with Hot Chai (page 172) 🏠
SATURDAY BREAKFAST	• Indian Scrambled Eggs (page 146)
SATURDAY LUNCH	• Mexican Chicken Wraps (page 151) 🏠
SATURDAY DINNER	• Campfire Chili Con Carne with Yogurt Guacamole & Tortilla Chips (page 157) • Banana Halwa (page 170) 🏠
SUNDAY BREAKFAST	• Sausage & Potato Hash (page 145)
SUNDAY LUNCH	• Chorizo & Chickpea Soup (page 148)

SHOPPING LIST

Spices & Flavorings
chicken bouillon cubes (2)
cumin, ground (1 tsp.)
garam masala (1½ tbsp.)
Hot Chai Mix (1 recipe
  quantity), (page 172)
olive oil (1 bottle)
salt & pepper
sugar, granulated (⅔ cup)

Cans & Jars
chickpeas (14½ oz.)
diced tomatoes (1 lb. 12 oz.)
kidney beans (14½ oz.)

Dry Foods
bread, crusty (½ loaf)
naan breads (6)

pistachios, shelled (2 tbsp.)
soft flour tortillas, large (4)
tortilla chips, lightly salted
  (1 large bag)

Meat
beef, ground (10½ oz.)
chicken breast filets (6)
chorizo, diced (9 oz.)
sausages, large (6)

Chilled Foods
butter (2¼ sticks)
cheddar cheese (14 oz.)
eggs, extra large (8)
milk (1 pint)
yogurt, thick plain
  (3½ cups)

Fruit & Vegetables
avocados (3)
bananas (6)
bell peppers, red (2)
chilies (4)
cilantro leaves (2 handfuls)
cucumber (1)
garlic cloves (8)
ginger root (1-in. piece)
limes (2)
onions, red (4)
parsley leaves (1 handful)
peaches (4)
potatoes, large (4)
Savoy cabbage (4 cups)
scallions (4)
tomatoes (2)

🍴 Meal Plan for Vegetarians

FRIDAY DINNER	• Halloumi & Vegetable Kebabs with Couscous Tabbouleh (page 166) 🏠 • Barbecued Peaches with Hot Chai (page 172) 🏠
SATURDAY BREAKFAST	• Breakfast Beans (page 147)
SATURDAY LUNCH	• Campfire Caponata with Garlic Bread (page 153) 🏠
SATURDAY DINNER	• Vegetable Biryani (page 165) • Banana Halwa (page 170) 🏠
SUNDAY BREAKFAST	• Indian Scrambled Eggs (page 146)
SUNDAY LUNCH	• Spaghetti Salad (page 152) 🏠

SHOPPING LIST

Spices & Flavorings
garam masala (2½ tsp.)
Hot Chai Mix (1 recipe
   quantity), (page 172)
olive oil (1 bottle)
red wine vinegar
   (⅔ cup)
salt & pepper
sugar, granulated (1 cup)
tomato ketchup (1 tbsp.)

Cans & Jars
cannellini beans
   (1 lb. 13 oz.)
capers (5 tbsp.)
chutney, mango (1 jar)
diced tomatoes
   (1 lb. 12 oz.)
olives, green pitted
   (1 cup)

Dry Foods
baguettes, large (2)
basmati rice (1¼ cups)
couscous (2⅓ cups)
naan breads (2)
pistachios, shelled
   (¾ cup)
spaghetti (14 oz.)

Chilled Foods
butter (2¼ sticks)
eggs, extra large (6)
halloumi cheese
   (1 lb. 2 oz.)
milk (1 pint)
yogurt, thick plain (2½ cups)

Fruit & Vegetables
bananas (6)
bell peppers, yellow (2)
celery heart (1)
cherry tomatoes (15)
chilies (2)
cilantro leaves (2 handfuls)
eggplants, large (2)
garlic cloves (9)
ginger root (1-in. piece)
lemons (2)
onions (4)
parsley leaves (3 handfuls)
peaches (4)
rocket leaves (1 handful)
scallions (4)
tomatoes (7)
vegetable mix, carrots,
   cauliflower, peas and
   zucchini (1 lb. 2 oz.)

Granola with Yogurt & Fruit

SERVES: 4
PREPARATION TIME: 15 MINUTES
COOKING TIME: ABOUT 10 MINUTES

¼ cup honey or light corn syrup, plus extra to serve
¼ cup sunflower oil, olive oil or butter
heaped 1½ cups rolled oats
½ cup nuts and seeds, chopped

½ cup shredded coconut
½ cup dried fruit, chopped
9 ounces fruit, such as strawberries or peaches, coarsely chopped, to serve

heaped 2 cups thick plain yogurt, to serve

1 Put the honey and oil in a large skillet. Put the pan over low heat and cook, stirring occasionally, about 2 minutes until hot and well combined.

2 Add the oats, nuts and seeds and coconut and toss gently but thoroughly until evenly coated. Shake the pan to evenly coat the bottom.

3 Put the pan over medium heat and cook about 6 minutes until golden, stirring frequently so the granola does not burn. Remove from the heat and let cool a little, then stir in the dried fruit.

4 Divide the fruit into bowls and spoon one-quarter of the yogurt over each portion. Serve sprinkled with granola and drizzled with honey.

 Prepare ahead: Make the granola at home before you leave. Preheat the oven to 375°F. Put all the dry ingredients, except for the dried fruit, and the hot honey and oil mixture on a baking sheet greased with oil. Toss well, then bake, tossing regularly, 15 to 20 minutes until golden. Let cool completely. Store in an airtight container up to 1 week.

Sausage & Potato Hash

This is a great morning-after-the-night-before meal. It's good kid fuel too, and everyone always wants more. It does take a little longer to cook if you increase the quantities to feed a hungry crowd. But it's well worth it!

SERVES: 4
PREPARATION TIME: 10 MINUTES
COOKING TIME: ABOUT 35 MINUTES

2 tablespoons olive oil, sunflower oil or butter, plus extra for frying if needed
1 large white onion or 2 red onions, finely sliced
6 large sausages, coarsely chopped
4 large potatoes, peeled and diced
1 handful of parsley leaves, coarsely chopped
2 extra large eggs, beaten
salt and pepper

1 Heat the oil in a skillet over low heat. Add the onion and cook about 10 minutes, stirring gently, until it starts to caramelize.
2 Put the pan over medium heat and add the sausages and potatoes. Cook, stirring occasionally, about 20 minutes until the sausages are cooked through and the potatoes are tender. Add a little more oil to the pan if needed.
3 Season to taste with salt and pepper and mix well. Stir in the parsley leaves and eggs and cook about 1 minute until the eggs are cooked. Serve hot.

Indian Scrambled Eggs

SERVES: 4
PREPARATION TIME: 10 MINUTES
COOKING TIME: ABOUT 15 MINUTES

6 extra large eggs
½ cup (¼ stick) butter,
  plus extra for spreading
  if needed
4 scallions, coarsely sliced
1-inch piece of ginger
  root, peeled and finely
  chopped
1 chili, seeded and
  chopped
2 tomatoes, diced

½ teaspoon garam masala
¼ teaspoon turmeric
  (optional)
2 handfuls of cilantro
  leaves, coarsely chopped
2 naan breads, cut in half
  or 4 pita breads
salt and pepper

1 Beat the eggs in a bowl and season with salt and pepper. Melt the butter in a saucepan over medium heat. Add the scallions, ginger and chili and cook about 2 minutes until golden. Add the tomatoes, garam masala and turmeric, if using, and cook 2 minutes longer.

2 Put the pan over low heat. Add the eggs and a pinch of salt and cook, stirring frequently, about 3 to 5 minutes until the eggs start to set. Stir in the cilantro leaves and continue cooking until the scrambled eggs are cooked to your liking. Remove from the heat, check the seasoning and add extra salt and pepper if needed.

3 Warm each naan bread over low heat on a portable barbecue or in a grill pan about 1 minute on each side. Serve warm with the scrambled eggs.

Breakfast Beans

This hearty breakfast is fantastic for feeding lots of hungry people. If you have no vinegar handy simply use 3 more tablespoons of tomato ketchup instead of the vinegar and sugar. You could also fry up some bacon to go with it.

SERVES: 4
PREPARATION TIME: 5 MINUTES
COOKING TIME: ABOUT 25 MINUTES

1 tablespoon olive oil or
   sunflower oil
1 onion, diced
heaped 1¾ cups canned
   diced tomatoes
1 tablespoon tomato
   ketchup
1 tablespoon red wine
   vinegar or white wine
   vinegar

2 tablespoons granulated
   sugar or brown sugar
1 teaspoon chili sauce
   (optional)
1 pound 13 ounces canned
   cannellini or other
   beans, drained
salt and pepper
sliced baguette or crusty
   bread, to serve

1 Heat the oil in a saucepan over medium heat. Add the onion and cook about 5 minutes until it starts to soften.

2 Add the canned tomatoes, ketchup, vinegar, sugar and chili sauce, if using, and season with salt and pepper. Cook about 15 minutes until the sauce has reduced and thickened.

3 Add the cannellini beans to the pan. Taste and season again with salt and pepper, if you like. Cook about 5 minutes until the beans have absorbed the heat and flavors of the sauce. Serve hot with slices of baguette.

Chorizo & Chickpea Soup

A healthy, but extremely filling lunch that is popular with all ages. And what's more, it's very simple to prepare. The quantities here are generous because you'll definitely want second helpings!

SERVES: 4
PREPARATION TIME: 5 MINUTES
COOKING TIME: ABOUT 20 MINUTES

heaped 1¾ cups canned
  diced tomatoes
5½ ounces chorizo, diced
4⅓ cups chicken stock

14½ ounces canned
  chickpeas, drained
5½ ounces Savoy cabbage,
  spinach, kale or chard,
  finely chopped

salt and pepper
crusty bread, to serve

1 Put the canned tomatoes in a saucepan and cook over low heat about 10 minutes until the juices have thickened.

2 Put the pan over high heat, then add the chorizo and stock and bring to a boil. Return the pan to low heat and simmer about 2 minutes to let the flavors combine and intensify.

3 Add the chickpeas to the pan and simmer 1 minute longer. Add the Savoy cabbage and season with salt and pepper to taste. Cook about 5 minutes until tender. Serve hot with crusty bread.

Mexican Chicken Wraps

SERVES: 4
PREPARATION TIME: 20 MINUTES, PLUS 10 MINUTES MARINATING
COOKING TIME: ABOUT 15 MINUTES

juice of 1 lime
2 garlic cloves, crushed
2 boneless, skinless
   chicken breast filets,
   cut into thin strips
1 large avocado, peeled
   and pitted

2 tablespoons thick plain
   yogurt
2 tablespoons olive oil or
   sunflower oil
1 red or white onion, sliced
1 red bell pepper, seeded
   and sliced

1 small chili, seeded and
   finely chopped or a
   splash of chili sauce
4 large soft flour tortillas
scant 1⅓ cups grated
   cheddar cheese
salt and pepper

1 Mix together the lime juice and garlic in a cup. Pour half of the mixture into a plastic freezer bag and reserve the other half. Add the chicken to the bag and seal. Let marinate in a cooler 10 minutes.

2 Add the avocado to the reserved lime and garlic mixture and mash with a fork until smooth. Stir in the yogurt, then season to taste with salt and pepper and set aside.

3 Heat the oil in a large skillet over medium-high heat. Add the onion, pepper and chili and cook about 5 to 10 minutes until softened and starting to brown. Add the chicken and marinade to the pan and season with salt and pepper. Cook about 5 minutes until the chicken is cooked through.

4 Spread one-quarter of the avocado mixture down the center of each tortilla, and top with one-quarter of the chicken mixture and one-quarter of the cheddar. Roll up the tortillas, tucking in one end, and serve warm. Use tinfoil to keep the wrap firmly together, if you like.

Prepare ahead: You could use ¼ cup Lime Marinade Base (page 21) instead of the lime juice and garlic. Make it at home before you leave.

Spaghetti Salad

This pasta dish is great to share and can be varied by adding approximately 1¾ ounces chopped salami or 3½ ounces canned tuna. It would also be good with 4½ ounces drained mozzarella. You might want to leave out the chili if you're feeding lots of little ones.

SERVES: 4
PREPARATION TIME: 8 MINUTES
COOKING TIME: ABOUT 10 MINUTES

14 ounces spaghetti
4 tomatoes, coarsely chopped and squashed
1 garlic clove, crushed
2 tablespoons capers, drained and rinsed

½ cup pitted green or black olives, coarsely chopped
1 handful of arugula leaves, coarsely chopped
a pinch of dried chili flakes or a splash of chili sauce (optional)

2 tablespoons olive oil
salt and pepper

1 Cook the spaghetti in plenty of salted boiling water until al dente. Drain well and return to the pan.
2 Add all of the remaining ingredients and toss gently but thoroughly. Check the seasoning and add a little extra salt and pepper if needed, but bear in mind the capers will be salty and the arugula will have an intense peppery flavor. Serve immediately.

 Prepare ahead: Combine all of the salad ingredients (except the spaghetti) at home before you leave. Store in an airtight container in a cooler up to 2 days. You could use 2 tablespoons of Marinade Base (page 21) instead of the garlic.

Campfire Caponata with Garlic Bread

SERVES: 4
PREPARATION TIME: 15 MINUTES
COOKING TIME: ABOUT 45 MINUTES

½ cup olive oil
2 large eggplants, cubed
1 teaspoon salt, plus extra
for seasoning
1 teaspoon dried oregano
(optional)
1 celery heart or 3 sticks,
cut into matchsticks

2 onions, sliced
heaped 1¾ cups canned
diced tomatoes
1 tablespoon sugar, any
variety
½ cup red wine vinegar
3 tablespoons capers,
drained and rinsed

½ cup pitted green olives,
halved
pepper

GARLIC BREAD:
1 large baguette, sliced
2 garlic cloves, crushed
½ cup (¼ stick) butter,
softened

1 Heat 6 tablespoons of the oil in a large skillet over medium heat. Add the eggplants and cook about 5 minutes until starting to brown. Add the salt and oregano, if using, and cook the eggplants 10 minutes longer until golden, turning frequently. Remove from the pan and drain on paper towels.

2 Add the remaining oil, celery and onions to the pan and cook about 5 minutes until softened and starting to turn golden. Add the canned tomatoes, sugar, vinegar and a pinch of salt, and simmer gently about 5 minutes. Return the eggplants to the pan and add the capers and olives. Cook over low heat about 5 minutes, then season to taste with salt and pepper. Cook 5 minutes longer until the caponata has thickened.

3 Meanwhile, make the garlic bread. Slice the baguette without cutting through the bottom crust, then mash together the garlic and butter and spread it over the cut sides of the baguette. Wrap in tinfoil and cook over medium heat on a portable barbecue or in a grill pan about 15 minutes until hot, moving the baguette from time to time so it doesn't burn. Serve hot with the caponata.

Prepare ahead: Make the caponata and garlic butter at home before you leave. Store in airtight containers in a cooler up to 4 days.

Classic Camping Burgers

SERVES: 4
PREPARATION TIME: 30 MINUTES
COOKING TIME: ABOUT 8 MINUTES

1 pound 10 ounces ground beef
1 onion, finely chopped, plus ½ onion, thinly sliced into rings, to serve (optional)
2 jarred or canned anchovy fillets, finely chopped
1 teaspoon pepper
2 handfuls of parsley leaves, chopped
4 burger buns, each cut in half horizontally
3½ ounces cheese, such as cheddar, Emmental or Gruyère, thinly sliced
salt and pepper
tomato ketchup, mayonnaise and mustard, to serve
4 crunchy lettuce leaves, to serve
1 large tomato, thinly sliced, to serve
4 pickles, thinly sliced, to serve

1 Put the ground beef, onion, anchovies, pepper and parsley leaves in a bowl and mix well. Using your hands, shape the mixture into 4 burgers. Cover and set aside.

2 Lightly toast the cut sides of the burger buns over low heat on a portable barbecue or in a grill pan about 1 to 2 minutes until crisp and lightly golden.

3 Just before grilling, season both sides of the burgers with salt and pepper. Grill over medium-high heat on a portable barbecue or in a grill pan about 2 minutes on each side for rare, about 3 minutes on each side for medium and about 4 minutes on each side for well done. Arrange the cheese slices on top of the burgers halfway through cooking to let the cheese melt slightly before serving.

4 Spread your choice of sauce over one half of each burger bun. Serve the burgers in the buns, with lettuce, tomato, pickles and onions, if you like.

 Prepare ahead: Mix together the ingredients for the burgers at home before you leave. Store in an airtight container in a cooler up to 1 day.

Campfire Chili Con Carne with Yogurt Guacamole & Tortilla Chips

SERVES: 4
PREPARATION TIME: 25 MINUTES
COOKING TIME: AT LEAST 1 HOUR 20 MINUTES

1 tablespoon olive oil or sunflower oil
1 onion, sliced
1 teaspoon ground cumin or dried oregano
1 red bell pepper, seeded and cut into large chunks
2 garlic cloves, finely chopped
3½ ounces chorizo, diced
1 chili, seeded and finely chopped (optional)

10½ ounces ground beef
heaped 1¾ cups canned diced tomatoes
14½ ounces canned kidney beans, drained
salt and pepper
heaped 2 cups grated cheddar cheese, to serve
1 large bag of lightly salted tortilla chips, to serve

YOGURT GUACAMOLE:
2 avocados, peeled and pitted
¼ cup thick plain yogurt
1 tablespoon olive oil
juice of ½ lime
1 garlic clove, crushed
salt and pepper

1 Heat the oil in a large saucepan over medium heat. Add the onion and cook about 5 to 7 minutes until softened. Add the cumin, pepper, garlic, chorizo and chili, if using, and cook 1 minute longer.

2 Add the ground beef, season with salt and pepper and cook about 4 to 5 minutes until browned. Add the canned tomatoes and bring to a boil. Put the pan over very low heat, cover with a lid and cook gently at least 1 hour, preferably 2 hours. If you are cooking on an open fire, only partially cover the pan (this will give the dish a wonderful smoky flavor.)

3 Meanwhile, make the yogurt guacamole. Put all of the ingredients in a bowl and coarsely mash with a fork. Season to taste with salt and pepper.

4 Add the kidney beans to the pan about 10 minutes before the end of the cooking time. Serve hot with grated cheese, guacamole and tortilla chips.

Lamb, Eggplant & Mint Tagine

This recipe is deliberately heavy on the vegetables, as the eggplant is what makes the texture so rich and delicious. However, it is equally good with more meat and less eggplant if you prefer it that way.

SERVES: 4
PREPARATION TIME: 15 MINUTES
COOKING TIME: AT LEAST 1¼ HOURS

6 tablespoons olive oil, plus extra if needed
2 eggplants, cut into bite-size pieces and lightly sprinkled with salt
2 onions, thinly sliced

14 ounces boneless lamb leg or shoulder, trimmed of fat and cut into bite-size pieces
1 teaspoon cinnamon
1 teaspoon ground allspice

3¼ cups canned diced tomatoes
2 handfuls of mint leaves, chopped
salt and pepper
cooked couscous or rice, to serve

1 Heat ¼ cup of the oil in a large heavy-bottomed saucepan over medium heat. Pat the eggplants dry with paper towels, wiping away any excess salt. Working in batches if necessary, cook the eggplants about 10 minutes until golden, adding more oil to the pan if needed. Remove the eggplants from the pan and set aside.

2 Put the pan over medium-low heat and add the remaining oil. Add the onions and cook about 10 minutes until softened and golden.

3 Add the lamb and spices and season with salt and pepper. Cook about 5 minutes until the lamb is starting to brown, then return the eggplants to the pan and add the canned tomatoes. Season with salt and pepper and bring to a boil over medium heat. Cover with a lid, put the pan over low heat and simmer gently at least 40 minutes, preferably 1 hour, until the tagine has thickened and the lamb is meltingly tender.

4 Stir in the mint leaves about 5 minutes before serving to let the mint infuse. Serve hot with couscous.

Sticky Ribs with Corn on the Cobs

SERVES: 4
PREPARATION TIME: 10 MINUTES, PLUS AT LEAST 1 HOUR MARINATING
COOKING TIME: ABOUT 25 MINUTES

2 racks of pork ribs (about
  12 to 14 ribs)
4 corn on the cobs,
  husks on
salt and pepper
butter, to serve

STICKY MARINADE:
2 garlic cloves, crushed
2 tablespoons white wine
  vinegar
3 tablespoons honey or
  brown sugar
2 tablespoons tomato
  ketchup

1 tablespoon soy sauce
1 teaspoon chili sauce
  (optional)

1 To make the marinade, put all of the ingredients in a plastic freezer bag. Add the pork ribs and seal the bag. Let marinate in a cooler at least 1 hour, preferably overnight.

2 Soak the corn in cold water 20 minutes to prevent them from drying out during cooking. Cook the corn, in their husks or wrapped in tinfoil, in the glowing embers of a portable charcoal barbecue or open fire about 20 minutes until the kernels are tender. Alternatively, cook in plenty of boiling water about 5 to 10 minutes. Peel back the husks or tinfoil and season with salt and pepper.

3 Meanwhile, remove the ribs from the marinade and reserve the marinade. Season the ribs with salt and pepper and cook over medium heat on a portable barbecue or in a grill pan about 20 minutes, brushing from time to time with the reserved marinade and turning frequently, until crisp and cooked through. Serve hot with corn on the cobs smothered in butter.

Prepare ahead: Make the marinade at home before you leave and store in a cooler up to 1 week. You could even take the ribs in the marinade if you're planning to eat them on the first night.

Chicken Tikka with Cucumber Raita

SERVES: 4
PREPARATION TIME: 20 MINUTES, PLUS 10 MINUTES MARINATING
COOKING TIME: ABOUT 10 MINUTES

4 boneless, skinless
  chicken breast filets,
  cut into chunks
4 naan breads
salt and pepper

TIKKA MARINADE:
juice of ½ lime
3 garlic cloves, crushed
1 tablespoon garam masala
2 tablespoons thick plain
  yogurt
½ chili, finely chopped or
  1 teaspoon dried chili
  flakes

CUCUMBER RAITA:
1 cucumber, finely chopped
heaped 1 cup thick plain
  yogurt
1 handful of mint leaves,
  finely chopped (optional)
salt and pepper

1 If using wooden skewers, soak them in cold water at least 30 minutes before grilling. To make the marinade, put all of the ingredients in a plastic freezer bag. Add the chicken and seal the bag. Let marinate in a cooler 10 minutes.

2 Meanwhile, make the raita. Mix together the cucumber and yogurt in a bowl. Add the mint leaves, if using, and season to taste with salt and pepper.

3 Warm the naans over high heat on a portable barbecue or in a grill pan about 1 minute on each side. Wrap in tinfoil to keep them warm.

4 Remove the chicken from the marinade and reserve the marinade. Thread the chicken onto skewers, then season with salt and pepper. Cook over medium heat on a portable barbecue or in a grill pan about 6 to 7 minutes, brushing from time to time with the reserved marinade and turning frequently, until the juices run clear when the thickest part of the meat is pierced with the tip of a sharp knife or skewer. Serve hot with the raita and warmed naans.

Prepare ahead: Make the marinade at home before you leave and store in a cooler up to 3 days.

Crispy Smoked Paprika Chicken Wings

This is another great first-night dinner—easy to make and popular with the kids. Smoked paprika has a very distinctive flavor and a rich aroma, but don't worry if you don't have any—just use pepper instead.

SERVES: 4
PREPARATION TIME: 15 MINUTES, PLUS 15 MINUTES MARINATING
COOKING TIME: ABOUT 15 MINUTES

16 chicken wings
1 recipe quantity German
   Potato Salad (page 81),
   to serve

SMOKY MARINADE:
1 teaspoon smoked paprika
juice of 1 lemon or ¼ cup
   Marinade Base (page 21)
2 garlic cloves, crushed
½ teaspoon salt

1 To make the marinade, put all of the ingredients in a plastic freezer bag. Add the chicken wings and seal the bag. Let marinate in a cooler 15 minutes.
2 Remove the chicken wings from the marinade. Cook over medium-low heat on a portable barbecue or in a grill pan about 15 minutes, turning once, until the meat is beautifully charred and really crispy. If you're using a portable charcoal barbecue, cook the chicken over coals that have burnt down quite significantly to prevent the skin from burning. Serve hot with German Potato Salad.

🏠 Prepare ahead: Make the marinade at home before you leave and store in a cooler up to 1 week.

Keralan Coconut Fish Curry

SERVES: 4
PREPARATION TIME: 15 MINUTES
COOKING TIME: ABOUT 50 MINUTES

2 tablespoons sunflower oil
2 onions, finely sliced
4 garlic cloves, chopped
1-inch piece of ginger
root, peeled and finely
chopped (optional)
1 chili, seeded and finely
chopped or 1 teaspoon
dried chili flakes
2 handfuls of cilantro
leaves, chopped

1 tablespoon garam masala
or curry powder
heaped 1¾ cups canned
diced tomatoes
1¾ cups coconut milk
heaped 1 cup basmati rice
1 pound 12 ounces
boneless, skinless fish
fillets, such as hake or
pollock

9 ounces cooked jumbo
shrimp (optional)
juice of ½ lime or 2
tablespoons Marinade
Base, made with lime
juice (page 21)
salt and pepper
thick plain yogurt, to serve
mango chutney or eggplant
relish, to serve

1 Heat the oil in a large skillet over medium heat. Add the onions and cook about 10 minutes until softened. Add the garlic, ginger, if using, chili and half of the cilantro leaves and cook, stirring, about 2 to 3 minutes.

2 Add the garam masala and stir until thoroughly combined. Pour in the canned tomatoes and coconut milk and season with salt and pepper. Bring to a boil over high heat, then put the skillet over low heat and simmer gently about 20 to 30 minutes until the sauce has thickened.

3 Meanwhile, put the rice, a pinch of salt and scant 2 cups water in a saucepan and bring to a boil over high heat. Cover with a lid, put the pan over low heat and cook about 10 minutes until all the liquid has been absorbed and the rice is tender.

4 Add the fish to the sauce and gently stir. Cook about 5 minutes until a skewer inserted into the thickest part of the flesh meets no resistance. Stir in the shrimp, if using, and cook about 2 to 3 minutes until hot.

5 Just before serving, stir in the lime juice and the remaining cilantro leaves. Serve hot with the rice, yogurt and mango chutney.

Vegetable Biryani

Biryanis are best when the rice crisps up on the sides and bottom of the pan, so don't worry about it sticking or even slightly browning. If you prefer chicken biryani, simply add four chicken breasts to the pan with the garam masala and a little extra seasoning, and cook 5 minutes until browned well on all sides.

SERVES: 4
PREPARATION TIME: 15 MINUTES
COOKING TIME: ABOUT 35 MINUTES

2 tablespoons (¼ stick) butter or sunflower oil
1 onion, sliced
2 garlic cloves, finely sliced
1 chili, seeded and finely sliced or ⅓ teaspoon dried chili flakes

2 teaspoons garam masala or curry powder
1 pound 2 ounces vegetable mix, such as zucchini, cauliflower, peas and carrots, cut into bite-size chunks

½ cup shelled pistachios, cashews or almonds
heaped 1 cup basmati rice
salt and pepper

1 Heat the butter in a large saucepan over medium heat. Cook the onion about 5 minutes until softened. Add the garlic and chili and cook, stirring, about 2 to 3 minutes, then add the garam masala and stir until thoroughly combined.

2 Add the vegetables to the pan and season with salt and pepper. Cover with a lid and cook about 4 minutes. Remove the lid, add the nuts and cook 1 minute longer.

3 Add the rice and a pinch of salt and stir gently until well mixed. Pour in 2 cups water and bring to a boil over high heat. Cover with a tight-fitting lid, put the pan over very low heat and cook, without stirring, about 15 minutes until all the liquid has been absorbed and the rice is starting to crisp up. Remove from the heat and let stand, covered, 10 minutes. Serve hot.

Halloumi & Vegetable Kebabs with Couscous Tabbouleh

SERVES: 4
PREPARATION TIME: 15 MINUTES
COOKING TIME: ABOUT 10 MINUTES

1 pound 2 ounces halloumi cheese, cut into bite-size pieces
2 yellow or red bell peppers, seeded and cut into bite-size pieces
6¼ ounces cherry tomatoes
olive oil, for drizzling

COUSCOUS TABBOULEH:
heaped 2 cups couscous
3 handfuls of parsley leaves, finely chopped
1 tomato or 4 cherry tomatoes, finely chopped
salt and pepper

LEMON & GARLIC DRESSING:
juice of 2 lemons and 4 garlic cloves, crushed or ½ cup Marinade Base (page 21)
¼ cup olive oil
salt and pepper

1 If using wooden skewers, soak them in cold water at least 30 minutes before grilling. Put the couscous in a large bowl and pour over scant 2½ cups boiled water. Season with salt and pepper and cover immediately. Let soak at least 5 minutes until the grains are tender.

2 Thread the halloumi, peppers and cherry tomatoes alternately onto skewers. Drizzle each skewer with oil and cook over high heat on a portable barbecue or in a grill pan about 6 minutes, turning from time to time, until browned.

3 Meanwhile, make the dressing. Mix together all of the ingredients in a bowl and season to taste with salt and pepper.

4 Fluff up the couscous with a fork, then add the parsley leaves, tomato and half of the dressing and mix well. Serve the kebabs with the couscous and with the remaining dressing drizzled over the top.

 Prepare ahead: Make the dressing at home before you leave and store in a cooler up to 1 week.

Chocolate Fondue

You can serve pretty much any type of fruit with this dessert, but we love strawberries, raspberries, pears, bananas, grapes, dried apricots and dried apple slices. For our children chocolate fondue is a camping must, especially when we're camping with other families. They love sitting in a circle and sharing with their friends—and the chocolate gets everywhere!

SERVES: 4
PREPARATION TIME: 5 MINUTES
COOKING TIME: ABOUT 10 MINUTES

7 ounces chocolate, any variety, broken into squares

1 pound 2 ounces mixed fresh or dried fruit, cut into bite-size pieces

1 bag of marshmallows

1 Put the chocolate in a heavy-bottomed saucepan over very low heat. Stir continuously until the chocolate has melted, then remove the pan from the heat.

2 Encourage everyone to spear fruit and marshmallows onto forks and skewers before dipping them into the gooey chocolate fondue. If the chocolate begins to harden, briefly return the pan to the heat.

Banana Halwa

Bananas are such great camping food, and this recipe is particularly good because the halwa can be kept wrapped up unrefrigerated for a couple of days. Nutritious and delicious!

MAKES: 4
PREPARATION TIME: 5 MINUTES
COOKING TIME: ABOUT 20 MINUTES

6 bananas, mashed
3 tablespoons sugar, any
   variety
1½ tablespoons butter
   (scant ¼ stick) or
   sunflower oil

2 tablespoons shelled
   pistachios or walnuts,
   chopped
thick plain yogurt or
   crème fraîche, to serve
   (optional)

1 Heat a skillet over medium heat. Add the bananas, sugar and butter and cook, stirring frequently, about 20 minutes until the bananas have browned and caramelized.

2 Remove the skillet from the heat and mix in the chopped nuts, then set aside and let cool a little. Using your hands, shape the halwa mixture into 4 golf-ball-size balls. Serve plain or with yogurt, if you like.

 Prepare ahead: Make the Banana Halwa at home before you leave. Wrap the balls in tinfoil or plastic wrap and store in an airtight container up to 2 days. Remember to let the balls cool completely before you wrap them up.

Camping Crepes

MAKES: 4
PREPARATION TIME: 10 MINUTES
COOKING TIME: ABOUT 10 MINUTES

CAMPING CREPES:
2 tablespoons (¼ stick)
  butter, plus extra for
  frying
1 cup all-purpose flour
¼ teaspoon salt
2 extra large eggs, beaten
generous 1¼ cups milk

TOPPING SUGGESTIONS:
bananas and honey
chocolate hazelnut spread
granulated sugar and
  lemon juice
ricotta cheese, granulated
  sugar and raisins

1 To make the crepes, melt the butter in a saucepan over low heat. Put the flour and salt in a large bowl. Make a well in the center of the flour mixture and add the eggs. Beat slowly with a fork to draw in the flour, then gradually beat in the milk to form a smooth batter. Stir in the melted butter.

2 Melt 1 tablespoon of butter in a skillet over medium heat, making sure it covers the bottom of the pan. Working in batches, pour 2 tablespoons of the batter into the pan to make a crepe, tilting the pan to make sure the batter evenly covers the bottom.

3 Cook about 30 seconds to 1 minute on each side until golden. Transfer the crepe to a plate and wrap in tinfoil to keep it warm. Repeat with the remaining batter, adding more butter to the pan as needed.

4 Top each crepe with fillings of your choice, then roll them up and serve warm.

Prepare ahead: Make the crepes at home before you leave. Let cool completely, then stack between sheets of parchment paper, wrap in tinfoil and store in a sealed plastic freezer bag in a cooler up to 3 days. To reheat a crepe, melt 1 tablespoon of butter in a skillet over low heat and cook about 30 seconds on each side until heated through.

Barbecued Peaches with Hot Chai

SERVES: 4
PREPARATION TIME: 5 MINUTES
COOKING TIME: ABOUT 25 MINUTES

generous 1½ cups milk
4 peaches
¼ cup granulated sugar or
   honey, to serve
thick plain yogurt, crème
   fraîche or ice-cream, to
   serve

HOT CHAI MIX:
6 cloves
2 cinnamon sticks
6 black peppercorns
½ nutmeg, grated
8 teaspoons granulated
   sugar
4 teaspoons black tea
   leaves

1 To make the chai, pour the milk and generous 1½ cups water into a heavy-bottomed saucepan. Warm over medium heat 3 to 5 minutes, then add the Hot Chai Mix. Bring to a boil, then put the pan over low heat and simmer gently about 10 to 20 minutes until the color deepens. The longer you leave the mixture to simmer, the stronger the taste becomes.

2 Meanwhile, cook the peaches over high heat on a portable barbecue or in a grill pan, turning occasionally, about 8 to 10 minutes until chargrilled and golden on the outside and soft on the inside.

3 When the chai is ready, pour into mugs, straining out as much of the spice mixture as possible with a large spoon. Sprinkle sugar over the peaches and serve with yogurt and a mug of hot chai.

 Prepare ahead: Combine the Hot Chai Mix at home before you leave. Store in a sealed plastic freezer bag up to 1 month.

Index

PICTURE ACKNOWLEDGMENTS:

Key:
l = left, r = right, a = above, b = below
Ed Easton / © Duncan Baird Publishers: 10(b), 31, 34, 37, 40, 43, 46, 49, 52, 55, 58(bl & br), 62, 67, 68, 73, 74, 79, 80, 85, 86, 91, 92, 100, 105, 108, 111, 112, 117, 118, 123, 124, 129, 130, 138, 143, 144, 149, 150, 155, 156, 161, 162, 167, 168, 173.
Jim Easton: 26.
Tiff Easton: 2, 10(a), 11, 18, 22, 23, 58(al & ar), 59, 96, 97, 134, 135, 174, 175.